COACHING
IN
ORGANIZATIONS

Best Coaching Practices from
The Ken Blanchard Companies

by
MADELEINE HOMAN BLANCHARD, MCC
&
LINDA J. MILLEF

D1446018

For Ken, Margie, and Scott Blanchard,
for your confidence in and commitment to coaching.

Contents

Foreword

EVER SINCE I WROTE *Everyone's a Coach* with Hall of Fame football coach Don Shula, I've been impressed by the difference a good coach can make for a sports team. Yet it wasn't until our son, Scott Blanchard, got excited about coaching and its impact on our field that I started to realize how effective organizational coaching can be in helping everyone close the gap between what they know and what they actually do.

When Scott and Madeleine started Coaching.com with the vision of making it easy for organizations to offer coaching, I was a big staunch supporter. To increase my understanding of the coaching field, they insisted that I have my own coach. Realizing that I could be a slippery character, they asked Shirley Anderson—one of the premier coaches in our field—to take me on. Not only has working with Shirley been a joy, it also has led to a breakthrough in closing the learning/doing gap, a problem that has frustrated me for a long time. Allow me to explain.

Over the years I found that everybody was excited about The Ken Blanchard Companies' leadership training, but too few were putting their new knowledge into practice in a way that really made a difference in their lives and the lives of those they touched. When we began to incorporate coaching into our training, the feedback and results were remarkable. People were actually using what they'd learned. For companies that agree to give follow-up coaching to their people after training, the benefits far outweigh the cost. That is why *Coaching in Organizations* is a welcome and timely addition to business literature.

Coaching has arrived as a human development tool, and is here to stay. Because Madeleine and Linda love to see people reach their potential, they are on a mission to share this powerful tool more widely. They have been working as coaches in organizations for over a decade, improving the lives of more than 3,000 people in more than 100 companies, from privately held firms to Fortune 100s. In addition, they have partnered with and managed more than 200 coaches, delivering coaching services through their own companies as well as The Ken Blanchard Companies. By sharing their experiences—with an emphasis on best practices, learning from mistakes, and an honest reporting of what works and doesn't work—they have made a significant contribution to this important new field.

This book is the how-to coaching manual we've all been waiting for. Thanks, Madeleine and Linda. We really need coaching in organizations. My hope is that everyone who reads this book will learn valuable information that positively impacts their careers and the success of their organizations.

—KEN BLANCHARD
Co-author of *The One-Minute Manager*
and *Leading at a Higher Level*

Acknowledgments

THIS BOOK IS THE CULMINATION of years of trial and error with people who have been our partners, our colleagues, and, in some cases, our guinea pigs.

Thanks first to all the staff at The Ken Blanchard Companies: the leaders who invited us to be part of their coaching service offering, our sales professionals who trust us with their clients, and the project managers who took the leap of faith, even though they weren't sure about this "coaching thing." Special thanks to Scott Blanchard, our boss, who had the vision for democratizing coaching in organizations, for being a model of persistence and tenacity, and for making it easy for us to get things done.

We are only two members of a team that lives and breathes coaching. We learn together. We hold each other to a high standard. We cut each other slack when it's needed. And, we laugh *a lot*. Joni Wickline, who joined us at the inception of the organization, has been a tireless defender of best coaching practices. Someday her picture will be next to the word "efficient" in the dictionary. Patricia Overland, one of the first coaches to join us, has shown herself to be a true coaching leader. She keeps her head and her sense of humor in a crisis. Mary Ellen Sailer is as customer-focused as is humanly possible, and challenges us with her unique combination of heart and brains. Adam Morris, our rock, is insightful and hilarious. Everything we've learned, we've learned as a team. Being part of this team has been one of the most fulfilling experiences of our lives.

We are nothing without our coaches; they are the ones who deliver the goods, day after day. Thanks to each one for being worthy of the trust our clients place in us, for sharing what you learn, for your feedback and input. We set out to build an army of angels who champion and advocate for the best in each person, and you make us proud.

A very special thanks to our clients, who are extraordinary. We learn so much from every person we work with, and we appreciate each one. They are creative, analytical thinkers, phenomenally energetic, and a credit to their organizations. Each one has a service heart and makes every effort to do the best thing for his or her organization. We have laughed, cried, and partnered to get it right. Many of our clients have become our friends.

We love to work. Our families are kind to allow us to do just that. They know we can't help it. They gracefully tolerate our need to collaborate at odd times of the day and night, to design the finest content and offerings that we can, to make our clients happy, to write books. We are grateful to our husbands and our children for being our juggling partners in making it all flow.

Finally, enormous thanks and gratitude to Jenn Beverage for her beautiful work on the graphics and Margaret Dempsey ("Grit," to us) for her true genius of corralling our chaos. Grit has walked with us each step of the way, pushing us, challenging us to dig deeper, helping us pull together two diverse thinking and writing styles. Her brilliance and energy have been a fabulous gift to us.

Introduction

ORGANIZATIONS, both for-profit and not-for-profit, have realized that many challenges can be met with coaching. This book is written to support organizational service professionals with simple and easy tools to plan, implement, and manage coaching interventions.

The first few chapters are devoted to a broad overview of coaching in organizations—literally the basics. We will share a very brief consideration of where coaching came from and the environmental phenomena that provoked its (seemingly) sudden popularity. Then we will examine the key elements to keep in mind when considering the attempt to create a coaching culture in an organization. Business and HR leaders are asking, "Why can't our managers just be coaches? Why can't we shift our culture to be one of personal accountability, drive for performance and continuous learning?" This is a worthy goal, especially when more and more employees are seeking meaning and the opportunity for personal growth at work; and a coaching culture is key for individual growth. Yet, when organizations try to instill a coaching culture within their companies, they often encounter full-scale culture change with all of the attendant obstacles and glitches. We have seen a great deal of hard work undermined by lack of proper planning, inadequate support, or weak administration. Most have no idea what they have signed up for and are not prepared for the long haul.

Once we have addressed the big picture, we will narrow our focus to an analysis of the actual coaching experience that the individuals who receive coaching can have. Managing the coaching experience from concept through execution to conclusion and debrief is a team effort and will be critical to the success of the individual and the coaching engagement as a whole. It is amazing to us how many organizations investing hundreds of thousands of dollars in coaching are willing to leave to chance the coaching experience their valuable employees receive. This section will offer some mechanics on how to structure, implement, and manage the coaching experience.

Finally, Part One will conclude with an overview of the various ways of measuring ROI for any coaching implementation. There is a great deal of hope in organizations: hope that there is a silver bullet, a great new idea, a definitive answer to the question, "How can we prove that coaching and the development of our people on deep personal levels is a good use of our precious investment dollars?" What we've learned is that the result is only as good as the clarity and specificity with which the initial goals were set. To measure the results of coaching means starting with the end in mind and being satisfied with observable behavioral differences as experienced by the employees who surround the person being coached. For the data hungry, there are some other methods as well.

In Part Two of this book, we offer a more detailed handbook for the active practitioner of coaching. We will share a coaching process that works every time, along with basic skills that a novice can develop easily in the course of the work day. This will be helpful for the beginner, as well as for a group of seasoned coaches with different background and training seeking a common language.

Coaching is a broad tool—a means to various ends. We have devoted four separate chapters to an in-depth investigation into different kinds of coaching: their methodologies, tools, and potential results. The various ways that people in organizations are using coaching are divided into categories for the sake of discussion, though this is by no means an exhaustive list. These are simply the areas in which we see coaching being deployed to help organizations achieve their strategic business goals. They are:

- Coaching to Support Learning
- Coaching for Performance
- Coaching for Leadership Development—often referred to as Executive Coaching
- Team and Group Coaching

COACHING TO SUPPORT LEARNING

Training continues to be a billion-dollar business inside organizations. It often is the first resource considered when an employee expresses interest in continued development. However, reams of research show that once the training is completed, people migrate back to their old ways, sometimes even within 24 hours of the training![1]

Coaching to support learning is effective in keeping the training knowledge top-of-mind. When as few as three coaching sessions are offered as a follow-up to training, the training event is transitioned into a learning process. Surveys reveal that when participants in training classes know that there will be follow-up coaching sessions about how they are applying the training information, they are more inclined to apply the learning. Coaching to support learning becomes a form of accountability and a reinforcement tool that creates sustainability and ensures a real return on the invested training dollar.

COACHING FOR PERFORMANCE

Although performance coaching focuses on improving current performance or reviewing and learning from past performance of the person being coached, a distinction must be drawn between this type of coaching and performance management. Most organizations have performance management processes to use when a person is under-performing. Sometimes, it's the last step before a person is released from employment.

Coaching for performance is not for those situations. Instead, it focuses on improving performance for a valuable individual contributor who is motivated and committed to continuous development in the present job. This type of coaching may be less intense and delivered over less time, especially if the person is motivated. Coaching can have a profound impact when a person knows that he or she has personal value to the organization and that an investment is being made to help improve his or her performance.

COACHING TO SUPPORT LEADERSHIP DEVELOPMENT

Easily the oldest, most commonplace form of coaching, even this workhorse has undergone a transformation in the past five years. Although a scant few will receive coaching for remedial reasons, most executives get coaches because their jobs are too complicated for one head and they have no collegial or senior support. Many executives may become victims of technical success with too much time on the road, out of touch with their people and unaware of the impact that they make on others. Often, executive coaching is implemented to support a 360-degree feedback process in which an executive's senior leaders, colleagues, peers, and direct reports provide feedback about the individual's effectiveness by answering specific questions about behaviors. Many kinds of feedback instruments exist. Most focus on leadership and management competencies. Many companies have created their own feedback instruments based on the competencies they have established as the most crucial to business success. After all the feedback has been collected into a report, many individuals find it helpful to work with a coach to process and understand the implications of the results. Then, after a thorough debriefing, the executive can partner with a coach to create an action plan to help the executive re-tool day-to-day activities to become more effective and a better role model for employees. Experience shows that individuals are less likely to discount feedback and more likely to take useful action based on feedback when they have a coach to help them.

Development coaching, as distinct from performance coaching or performance management, is focused on an individual's future development. This type of coaching prepares a person for the next career move and may be needed on a longer basis than other types of coaching. This type of coaching takes a deeper look at the person, the trajectory, and the different types of growth needed. Development is the key to increased performance and enhanced career growth.

Many organizations are using coaching for leadership development of high potential, to build bench strength, to assist as leaders are moved to new positions, and to support their executives. There is a shortage of leaders looming on the horizon.

It is a well-accepted fact that the population growth rate for the United States is slowing. Between now and 2010, the U.S. population is projected to grow 1.1 percent annually, identical to the rate a decade earlier. After that, it will dip, eventually reaching 0.3 percent by 2030, even less by 2050.[2]

Senior leaders know that the future of their organizations is based on developing leaders. This is no small task. One global company conducted an internal study that revealed that the organization would be short approximately 1,200 leaders within 10 years. Organizational leaders recognized that they couldn't count on recruiting those leaders from outside the organization, which means that they would have to develop them from inside.

Leadership development is critical. Coaching can play a vital role in a variety of leadership settings.

TEAM AND GROUP COACHING

Several distinctions exist between a team and a group. Coaching works well for both types of communities, but there are a few crucial differences.

Team coaching can be powerful, particularly with a new or challenging project or deadline. Internal as well as external coaches who work with teams improve communication, foster commitment, and increase the likelihood of completing the project or goal.

Finally, in our last chapter we will offer an in-depth look at coaching competencies; the behaviors and habits necessary for a coach to be successful and to develop mastery. This chapter is designed to help HR professionals look for specific things when hiring or developing coaches for their organizations. We have shared some hard lessons we have learned over years of hiring coaches and deploying them with our valued clients—what to look for and what to avoid at all costs.

FORMS AND CHECKLISTS

Implementing a coaching program requires an enormous amount of planning and communication. A sponsor and manager of any coaching program will need to possess (or develop!) the organizational abilities of a mobilizing field marshal. To that end we have provided checklists, sample communication templates, and process maps throughout the book. The final appendices contains a template for a coaching handbook and a sample of an impact report used to establish ROI. The names and details will all need to be changed for use in your organization, but should provide a launching pad at the very least.

The research is conclusive. People who receive great coaching love it and credit coaching with making a significant impact on important decisions and quality of life at work and home. Companies that hire coaches to work with their employees continue to experience observable return on investment even if they have not invested in formal ROI studies. Coaching, once thought of as a fad, seems to be here to stay. This book was written from the passionate desire to provide coaching on a large scale and bring relief to hundreds of employees at a time while increasing performance within organizations. We hope it will help put order to chaos, answers to questions, and better questions where there were none.

NOTES

1. Helpful reports on this research include: MCGovern, Lindemann, Vergara, Barker, Murphy, Barker, Warrenfeltz, "Maximixing the impact of executive coaching: behavioral change, organization outcomes, and return on investment" *The Manchester Review,* (2001, No. 6): 1–9; as well as Neil Rackham, *Training and Development Journal,* (November 1979, No. 1):12–16.
2. Robert J. Grossman, *HR Magazine,* March, 2005. See SHRM Website: http://www.shrm.org/hrmagazine/articles/0305/0305covstory.asp

PART I

The Basics of Organizational Coaching

CHAPTER 1

The History and Context of Coaching

EVERY DAY IN EVERY COMPANY, people are being hired, promoted, or moved from one position to another. Every day in every company, people need development as part of their ongoing professional growth. Every day in every company, people look to training as one of the most effective ways to give people skills and tools in organizations. But training is only one way to bridge developmental gaps.

The acquisition, development, and retention of good people are recognized by many fine organizations as obvious competitive advantages. Coaching has emerged as a powerful discipline that organizations are leveraging in various ways to build and retain their people. Coaching is a relative newcomer to organizations. As recently as the late 1980s, coaching was focused primarily on individual athletics and team sports. Coaching as an application to help individuals achieve better results in areas other than sports emerged from several sources simultaneously:

- Ontological philosophy, which questions the very nature of being.
- Organizational, cognitive, behavioral, and "positive" psychology, which examine the questions of how people function in groups, how people learn and change, and what makes people feel happy or satisfied.

- Theater performance, which might be defined as the ability to project a fabricated reality, and which implies the mastery of the art of "presence."
- Business consulting paradigms, which teach managers and leaders the mechanics of successful business.
- Social anthropology, which examines how different cultures define success and how leaders are chosen.
- Even neuroscience, which, in the context, studies how brain structure and chemistry affect a person's ability to change and grow.[1]

Ultimately, the disciplines that add to the vast store of knowledge that helps coaches be effective all share the same root: the way in which humans develop, relate to others, and grow and change in order to better achieve their goals.

Today, at least half of the Fortune 1000 organizations are providing coaching for their employees in one form or another. In a survey of members of the Institute for Executive Development, 59 percent of respondents said that the budget for coaching in their organizations would increase by more than 10 percent annually moving forward, despite only 7 percent stating they have a formal process to measure and calculate the return on investment (ROI) of the coaching.

An article in the *London Times*[2] revealed that British cabinet ministers and other civil servants across several governmental departments are receiving coaching at taxpayers' expense. The coaching is helping government leaders analyze complex issues, think more creatively, and manage life/work balance more effectively. Of course, considerable hue and cry have been heard from the opposing party about the practice, which has been a source of mockery and derision among a public that is largely misinformed about what coaching really is.

Great debate continues to swirl among professional coaches from all different backgrounds about what coaching really is and how it should be done. The resulting confusion has made it extraordinarily difficult for human resources (HR) and organizational development (OD) professionals and managers in organizations to define coaching, to find a reasonably simple coaching model, and to implement the use of coaching in their organizations with any confidence. Most organizations are too bottom-line-focused to allow for trial and error.

Coaching in Organizations is designed to share what we've learned as coaching practitioners working with professionals in organizations to deploy coaching easily, effectively, and, most importantly, with impact. The book is not intended to serve as a comprehensive overview of all coaching done by all coaches in all organizations everywhere. Nor is it intended to be a compendium of all empirical research done on coaching. Rather, it is an account of what we've learned working as coaching practitioners in organizations. It is written for HR, OD, and leadership development professionals who are tasked with introducing, managing, or measuring the effect of coaching in organizations.

A DEFINITION OF COACHING

We receive three to five calls a week from friends of friends and colleagues of friends, who ask: "I need to provide coaching to the sales force. Where do I start?" "I have been asked to centralize all the coaching that's going on in the organization and make sure it is consistent. Do you have some guidelines?" "Our board of directors wants to know how we know that the investment in coaching is paying off. I have some ideas, but I wonder what you guys are doing."

The best place to begin to answer those questions is to define the term *coaching*, for confusion in this regard abounds. If one were to ask 10 separate coaching professionals for their definitions, at least 10 answers would result. Table 1.1 contains a number of variations.

Table 1.1

Various Definitions of Coaching

A person who trains or directs athletes or athletic teams; a person who gives instruction, as in singing or acting; a private tutor employed to prepare a student for an examination.	*The American Heritage Dictionary*
Helping successful leaders achieve positive, lasting change in behavior: for themselves, their people and their teams	Marshall Goldsmith[3]
An informed dialogue whose purpose is the facilitation of new skills, possibilities, and insights in the interest of individual leading and organizational advancement.	Terry Bacon and Kevin Spear[4]
A comprehensive communication process in which the coach provides performance feedback to the coachee. Topics include broad, work relations dimensions of performance (personal, interpersonal or technical) that affect the coach's ability and willingness to contribute to meaningful personal and organizational goals.	Thomas Crane[5]
A collaborative solution-focused, results-oriented, and systematic process in which the coach facilitates the enhancement of work performance, life experience, self-directed learning, and personal growth of the coach.	Anthony M. Grant[6]
Unlocking a person's potential to maximize his or her own performance.	John Whitmore[7]
The art of facilitating the unleashing of people's potential to reach meaningful, important objectives.	Phillipe Rosinski[8]

In spite of the confusion, however, a few characteristics of the term seem to occur across the board:

Coaching:

- Is generally a one-to-one relationship.
- Usually involves development (of skills, awareness) and/or improved performance.
- Often involves gathering and sharing of feedback for the person being coached.
- Depends primarily on supportive rather than directive communication from the coach.

More specifically, for the purpose of this book, the following definition will be used. It has been honed by coaching practitioners in various organizational settings over a period of about five years.

> *Coaching is a* deliberate process *using* focused conversations *to* create an environment *for individual growth, purposeful action, and sustained improvement.*[9]

This definition is broad enough to enable multiple uses but narrow enough to identify the key components of a successful coaching relationship.

Many people think all they need to do to coach is to have great listening skills. Certainly, listening well is a key competency of a good coach; however, it is only one of many. Good coaching is not a random set of activities; rather, it involves using the same mechanics for every kind of conversation (performance, goal setting, career development, leadership, vision, strategy), because a number of solid mechanics work well consistently.

All coaching is a dialogue of some sort, whether it happens over email, voice mail, or face to face—in synchronous time or over a period of time. The coach is responsible for creating an environment in which the person being coached will learn, grow, act, perform, and behave differently in some way that will significantly enhance that individual's success at reaching personal long- and short-term goals. How the coach creates this environment is radically different for each client and is at the root of the mystery that surrounds the process of coaching.

In addition to the aforementioned mechanics, there is also an art to achieving this with every client, day after day, year after year. Finally, coaching is a *service*. Successful coaches are willing and able to show up and be fully present with each client, stay free of their own agendas, and modulate their own personalities and needs. Mediocre coaches are those who remain attached to their own opinions and feel the need to be right or even useful.

NOTE

Coaching competencies will be addressed in detail in Chapter 10.

WHY COACHING NOW?

The advent of coaching as a professional service to employees in organizations is the result of the confluence of several trends:

- *Advent of the "lean, mean machine."* Public companies are scrutinized routinely for waste. Poor performance is no longer tolerated; gone are the days the "likeable fixtures," or popular employees, are kept around out of sympathy. High performance is no longer an option, and organizations will invest in coaching support for people who add enough value.
- *No time for training.* Do you remember three- to five-day training events? Unless it relates to legal compliance for accounting or HR practices, time for training is being cut to the bone. Even so-called soft skills are being learned using online modules and virtual classrooms that don't require people to leave

the office. The cost is simply too high for employees to be away too long from their voice mail, email, and meetings.

Coaching is the perfect vehicle for precise, just-in-time learning. It takes much less time and can be scheduled at the employee's discretion. Coaching is also an excellent way to capitalize on whatever training has been done, as people who are coached posttraining are vastly more likely to apply their knowledge and adopt new behaviors than those who aren't.[10]

- *The vanished middle manager.* A new term has emerged from this trend: the *working manager.* This means that employees are responsible for providing adequate amounts of information, accountability, direction, support, and all the HR compliance record-keeping for large numbers of people while also doing a full-time "individual contributor's job." This trend is prevalent in most organizations. Coaches can provide what some managers can't or won't—specific skills improvement, sustained focus, a safe place for deep personal reflection, and sometimes much-needed empathy and attention. Coaches are filling in the space left open by inexperienced or overloaded managers.

- *Increased pace of business.* The speed at which business is conducted today has accelerated and continues to do so. The prediction in the 1970s that new technologies would help get work done more efficiently and leave people with more leisure time is, now, laughable. All these technologies have done is to enable one person to do the work of several. And, as the pace of work increases, so does the pace of change. Thus, the need for people to be able to manage their inner lives and adapt to change is critical. Coaches can offer perspective and help employees structure their time and prioritize their activities more effectively.

- *"Turbo leader" development.* Related to the speed of business is the time it takes for young talent to rise to leadership positions—usually long before they have had time to reflect on and synthesize their own experiences. Coaches can help with targeted work in the crucial areas of vision, purpose, and "knowledge and use of self."[11]

- *The "me generation."* Young people in organizations feel that they are special and unique. They respond favorably to a service that is tailored specifically for them. In addition, in exchange for working 24/7, younger workers expect to be developed; many see it as a right. Employees regard coaching as a perk and an acknowledgment that they are valuable enough for the investment.

COACH TRAINING PROGRAMS

How can one tell if a coach has been well trained? Simple! Sit in on the first three minutes of a coaching session with that coach. Companies that hire coaches to deliver services are in unanimous agreement: Consultants and psychologists who serve as coaches, thinking that their current levels of experience and knowledge will serve with no additional coach training, are finding it harder and harder to get by. Not even business experience, advanced degrees, and a deep knowledge of psychology and counseling are enough to prepare one for the rigors of coaching in organizations. The demand for real results is simply too strong, and coaches must know exactly what they are doing at all times. Coach training is not optional.

Two phenomenal resources list coach training programs, with accompanying details about philosophical foundations and methodologies. The combination of these two sources will provide you an exhaustive overview.

- The Peer Resource Network website (www.peer.ca/coachingschools.html) is devoted to serving a vast network of coaches and other helping professionals. It contains a staggering amount of information. At the time of this writing, 225 coach training programs were listed.

- The International Coach Federation (www.coachfederation.
  org/ICF/For+Current+Members/Coach+Training/For+
  Prospective+Students/ACTP) lists more than 40 accredited
  coach training programs. The accreditation criteria are
  rigorous, indicating that these programs have existed for
  some time and have demonstrated clear standards. The site
  also lists programs that offer accredited training hours.

COACHING ASSOCIATIONS

Googling the term *coaching organization* yields more than
6,500,000 matches. Over the past five years, coaching organizations have cropped up like mushrooms after a rainstorm, and
it has become increasingly difficult to know where to pay attention. We recommend the following three, on the basis of their
longevity, leadership stability, and support services: the International Coach Federation (ICF), the Professional Coaches and
Mentors Association (PCMA), and the Worldwide Association
for Business Coaches (WABC).

These organizations offer information, resources, an informed
and active community, and, in some cases, accreditation and
credentials. Following is a brief description of these top coaching
organizations.

THE ICF

In 1993, when the International Coach Federation formed, the
general public did not yet have access to the Internet; and, certainly, "google" was not yet in existence, much less used as a verb.
The ICF (www.coachfederation.org) was founded by Thomas
Leonard. Formed as a forward-thinking, open, and inclusive organization, its purpose was to answer the call from practicing
coaches who realized they needed an association to serve as a
source of community, information, standards, and ethics for the
profession. Several other professional organizations came into

being around the same time. Some folded together, and others continue individually to this day.

Today, the ICF is the world's largest professional association for coaches. As part of its scope of services, it:

- Establishes standards and ethics for coaches.
- Accredits coach training schools with clear criteria.
- Certifies coaches at three levels: Associate Certified Coach, Professional Certified Coach, and Master Certified Coach.
- Offers annual international coaching conferences, annual executive coaching summits, and annual research symposiums.
- Provides structure and support for a worldwide network of chapters designed to support coaches with community and continuing education.

Although some coaches argue that there is no standardization[12] in the coaching profession, the credentialing, ethics, and standards established by the ICF are rigorous and reliable for basic coaching skills. True, coaching for the development of managers, leaders, and executives has yet to be strictly codified. In fact, the efforts of the ICF to accredit coach training organizations and create standards for coaches recognized by a credential have generated criticism that the organization has become exclusive, despite its original vision of openness. Only time will tell whether the ICF will weather the storm that is sure to break over licensing, credentialing, and legal implications for coaches. Still, each year, a higher percentage of organizations are requesting that the coaches staffed on their projects be ICF-certified.

THE PCMA

Established in the early 1990s, the Professional Coaches and Mentors Association (www.pcmaonline.com) has a similar mission to, but with a broader audience base than, the ICF because it includes both coaches and mentoring professionals. The PCMA retains its original mission of openness and inclusiveness. Based in California, the organization has chapters primarily in that state and hosts an annual conference there as well.

THE WABC

The Worldwide Association for Business Coaches (www .wabccoaches.com/index.htm), founded in 1997, focuses strictly on the business coaching niche and has the distinction of being the only international association dedicated solely to serving the business coaching industry. Interestingly, it is also one of the few for-profit associations for coaches, and has a fairly new charismatic leader, Wendy Johnson. This group offers conferences worldwide and is currently working on accreditation for training programs.

As organizations are becoming more aware of the benefits of coaching, they are seeking well-trained, professional coaches to work within their walls. Many are already asking about ICF accreditation and are committed to working with coaches who are equipped as proficient organizational coaches.

NOTES

1. David Rock and Jeffrey Shwartz, "Breakthroughs in Brain Research Explain How to Make Organizational Transformation Succeed," *Strategy & Business*, No. 43, July 2006, Reprint # 06207 (to locate reprint, go to http://www.strategy-business.com/search/archives/?issue=& textfield=06207).
2. Isabel Oakeshott, "Call My Life Coach, Not a Spin Doctor," *London Times* Online, http://www.timesonline.co.uk/tol/news/uk/article620837.ece; August 27, 2006.
3. Marshall Goldsmith, via email, in response to personal correspondence. January 9, 2007.
4. Terry Bacon and Karen Spear, *Adaptive Coaching* (Palo Alto, CA: Davies-Black Publishing, 2003), xvi.
5. Thomas Crane, *The Heart of Coaching* (San Diego, CA: FTA Press, 1998), 31.

6. Anthony M. Grant, *International Journal of Evidence-Based Coaching and Mentoring*, "October 2002, the UK College of Life Coaching established the first International Coaching Summit," Vol. 1, No. 1, August 2003, http://www.brookes.ac.uk/schools/education/ijebcm/ijebcm-docs/vol1-no1-conference-review.pdf. Note that Dr. Grant has generated multiple definitions of coaching since the publication of this article; this one is used as an example.

7. John Whitmore, *Coaching for Performance* (London: Nicholas Brealey Publishing, 2002), 8.

8. Phillipe Rosinski, *Coaching Across Cultures* (London: Nicholas Brealey Publishing, 2003), 4.

9. Linda Miller and Madeleine Homan, *Coaching Essentials for Leaders* (The Ken Blanchard Companies, 2002), 4.

10. Neil Rackham, *Training and Development Journal*, "The Coaching Controversy" November 1979, No. 11: 12–16.

11. Term coined by Scott Blanchard for Blanchard Coaching Management System, 2000.

12. Alyssa Freas, "The Wild West of Executive Coaching," *Harvard Business Review*, November 1, 2004: Reprint No. O411E.

CHAPTER 2

Creating a Coaching Climate in Your Organization

COMPANIES NOW RECOGNIZE the power of coaching at the individual or team level, and so are offering coaching skills training to key leaders and managers, and include coaching as one of their leadership competencies or strategic initiatives to ensure that it permeates their corporate environments. This chapter is for people in organizations who want to infuse coaching into their corporate culture, thereby creating a coaching climate. Included here is information about what constitutes a coaching climate, and how to create one, as well as information about preparing internal coaches to deliver coaching to internal leaders and managers.

Note that there is no cookie-cutter approach to creating a coaching climate, as every organization is different. Therefore, the information is offered as guidelines and food for thought, and poses key questions to answer by the individual organization.

Making It Real

- How open to coaching is your organization?
- Which aspects of your organization could coaching impact in a positive way?

WHAT IS A COACHING CLIMATE?

When an organization has a coaching climate, interactions and conversations are different from those without this environment. The emphasis is on development, learning, and growth. Instead of being reluctant to admit that something didn't go well, people are willing to "tell on themselves," suggest solutions, and share what they've learned. And rather than people feeling they must defend their position or blame others for failures, they take responsibility for their actions and seek to learn from their mistakes. No longer do employees shrink from challenging projects; instead they feel empowered to step up, knowing that others will help them be successful.

More, a coaching climate is a culture where people have the skills, and are given permission, to have timely, relevant conversations about growth, development, performance, tasks, and goals. It's a feedback culture, where there are few surprises.

BELIEVING OTHERS TO BE CAPABLE

To shift to a coaching climate, it's important to be aware of what people believe about themselves and others. Most individuals come into organizations with the attitude that they have to prove themselves by excelling in all that they do. To that end, they attempt to become experts, and may feel threatened if others can do the job as well as, or better than, they can. Sometimes, people even reject help or sabotage coworkers who might be seen as more competent than they are. This, obviously, can create an environment of competitiveness, finger-pointing, blaming, micromanaging, or inappropriate delegation of tasks. This kind of environment erodes trust and is the opposite of one that fosters collaboration, development, and learning.

> Welcome to BCD, Inc., a company where people are focused on learning, developing themselves and others, and growing. Employees in this company believe that others are capable of making

good decisions; they collaborate as often as possible, and are open and creative in finding new options and solutions. Even when people are new to a task or goal and need direction, coworkers are confident that the person will become capable, collaborative, and creative. This is an example of an organizational culture that inspires trust and respect, confidence and mutuality, resourcefulness and innovation.

Attitudes That Signal a Coaching Climate

- People are seen as capable.
- Development is as important as deadlines.
- Mistakes are regarded as opportunities for learning.
- Feedback is given with a focus-forward orientation.

What's so important about these shifts? They make it possible to see the potential in others and then to commit to helping them fulfill it. When organizations can embrace these shifts, they are on the way to a coaching climate.

Making It Real

- How collaborative is your organization?
- What differences do you notice in divisions or teams where collaboration is the norm as compared to divisions or teams where it is not?
- What can you do to increase collaboration in your area of the company?

EMPHASIZING DEVELOPMENT AND MEETING TARGETS AND DEADLINES

Within a coaching climate, there is always a focus on opportunities to develop others, in addition to an emphasis on goals, targets, deadlines, and the bottom line. Within a coaching climate, all these can be achieved.

Focusing only on goals, targets, deadlines, and the bottom line often puts people into short-term thinking and crisis mode. There's always something else that comes up to take the attention away from long-term development of others. But there's a high price to pay for not taking the time to develop others. It's the amount of time you have to do things that others could be doing, rather than doing those things only you can do.

Think about the person who comes in with the same or similar situations repeatedly. About the times that others could be making decisions but aren't. About the potential creativity and new ideas that might be generated if others were invited into problem solving. Sure, it takes time to develop others to make decisions, to figure things out on their own, to become proficient in problem solving. Yet the time spent in developing others is time that one day will be all yours!

> Jeanette is a midlevel manager who oversees a production line in a manufacturing company. She has seven direct reports; five are managers, two are not. When Jeanette became aware of coaching, she realized that she solves most of the problems that her team brings into her office. She knows that her team has the capability and needs to be making many of the decisions and coming up with their own solutions.
>
> Recently, she started to think about how much time she could save if she weren't taking on what others could do. This recognition led her to become acutely aware of times when she is taking on responsibility unnecessarily rather than encouraging others to be more self-reliant.

What keeps leaders from taking the time to develop others? One reason may be that developing others isn't in the compensation structure. In most organizations, people are compensated for their key responsibility areas (KRAs), their key performance indicators (KPIs), their sales targets, and their specific and measurable deliverables. Developing people usually isn't on any of those lists.

In organizations that embrace coaching as part of the culture, this must change! Development of others must be tied into performance indicators and be compensated in new ways. The jury is still out on which organizations are going to be early adopters as they launch compensation structures that include developing others.

LEARNING FROM MISTAKES

How mistakes are handled is a distinct difference in teams or organizations with a coaching climate. In most companies, mistakes cost an employee credibility and trust. Someone is blamed. In contrast, in companies where coaching is part of the organizational dynamic, mistakes become opportunities for learning and growth. Taking responsibility for mistakes is expected.

During a recent conversation about the venue for a large meeting six months away, a VP determined that the designated venue would not work. Although plans had been made to use the facility, and a contract had been signed, no formal announcement had been made. When the VP first learned about the site, he immediately demanded answers: "Who made this decision? Why wasn't I consulted? How could you possibly think this was an adequate space?" The bombardment of questions served to blame and attack the person who had reserved the venue.

Had the same thing happened in a coaching climate, the questions might have started the same but led to a different set of questions: "Which parameters are needed for the meeting space? Where else can we meet? Who else can weigh in to be sure we have an adequate meeting space?"

In the first example, most of the questions are about the past. In the second example, most of the questions are focused on the future. In a coaching climate, when mistakes are made, the focus is on finding better options or solutions, instead of blaming and attacking those involved. This opens up an environment where people take responsibility for their errors, knowing that everyone will learn from them.

Making It Real

- How do you think about your own mistakes, or the mistakes made by others on your team?
- How is your perspective helpful or hurtful?
- What will you do to shift into even more useful thoughts or actions when a mistake is made?

GIVING FEEDBACK WITH A FOCUS-FORWARD ORIENTATION

Most leaders and managers dread feedback. They dread receiving it, and they really dread giving it. Normally, they delay dealing with it as long as possible. But as Ken Blanchard has said, "Feedback is the breakfast of champions." What does that mean? Given properly, in a timely manner, feedback can foster and inspire advanced development and growth in others. In organizations with a coaching climate, feedback becomes part of the fabric of teams and organizations, helping to create a safe environment where people trust each other and can be honest and timely when saying something doesn't work.

When a new team member, Sharon, joined Joan's team, Joan spent time with helping her understand what the team did and how the team operated. During the first team meeting that Sharon attended, a mistake was being discussed. Sharon jokingly made a comment to the team member responsible for the mistake, which unnecessarily embarrassed him. Joan was surprised. She had worked hard to create an environment of trust on her team, and she knew that comments like the one Sharon made did not fit with the team culture.

Within an hour after the meeting ended, Joan stopped by Sharon's office and said, "Something happened at the team meeting today that I'd like to discuss with you. When we were talking about the mistake that Larry made, I was surprised by your comment, even though it was made in jest. It seemed to say Larry was wrong. I'm not sure if I told you that we have some norms about how we treat others on our team, and one of them is that we don't intentionally make others wrong." As the conversation continued, Sharon became aware of how the team worked and what was expected during team meetings. She commented several months later to Joan that although the feedback had been difficult to hear, it was great to know that feedback would be immediate rather than withheld.

Many books are available that discuss feedback. Organizations with a coaching climate create a culture of ongoing, continuous feedback rather than withholding it. This means that feedback is offered any time, and is usually presented informally. When an organization or team declares that feedback is desired, and that its purpose is to help people to develop, feedback takes on an entirely different meaning and role.

With feedback as a daily part of the culture, employee reviews take on an entirely different function. Traditionally, reviews are used to look back at the past year (or six months) and discuss what worked and what didn't. When feedback is being given regularly, reviews become less relevant and necessary.

In a coaching climate, when annual meetings focus on what's ahead, they become *focus-forward* meetings. Unlike traditional reviews, focus-forward meetings look ahead to what is needed in the upcoming year. They emphasize the future, not the past. They set the bar on expectations around KPIs, KRAs, growth, and development for the year ahead, always focusing forward.

In addition, within focus-forward meetings, the conversation about job requirements is held in conjunction with development needs. Focus-forward conversations are excellent opportunities to brainstorm developmental activities that will help employees to accomplish their jobs and to develop themselves for their own career growth.

Making It Real

- What is your perspective on feedback?
- What needs to happen to make feedback a daily occurrence rather than a dreaded annual or semiannual activity?

LAUNCHING A COACHING CLIMATE

One of the most important components when launching a coaching climate is to make sure that messages about the importance of coaching come from the top level of the organization. Senior leaders need to be role models for coaching behaviors, and coaching needs to be closely linked to strategic business imperatives. Coaching competencies need to be added to performance competencies that are measured and rewarded. Although energetic managers can create pockets of coaching excellence in their own areas, the creation of a successful coaching climate company wide requires championing from the operational and strategic leaders.

FINDING LEADERSHIP STAKEHOLDERS

When launching a coaching climate, it's vital to determine who believes in coaching and is willing to speak to its value. Many leaders work with external coaches. One way to find out who the coaching advocates might be in your organization is to gather information, through informal conversations or surveys, about personal coaching experiences, asking specifically about benefits, the business case for coaching, and the impact on the leaders' ability to influence the organization.

If you send out a survey or talk with individuals to gather information, include questions that can help build a business case for coaching, such as:

1. As a leader, what were your reasons for working with an executive (or other type of organizational) coach?
2. What did you expect your coach to do with you?
3. What has happened since you started being coached, specifically, that has been most useful for you?
4. What has been the biggest surprise during your coaching?
5. What obstacles have you encountered during coaching?
6. How has coaching impacted your effectiveness as a leader?
7. What would make your coaching experience more effective?
8. What do you think about including coaching as a part of our culture?

In addition to surveys and informal conversations, another good place to find coaching advocates is on teams where coaching is being used on an ongoing basis. Such teams often are easily recognizable.

In a well-known Fortune 500 organization, the senior leader of one of the teams, Gene, was positively impacted by his first experience with coaching, and talked about it wherever he went. He was so influenced by it that he enrolled in a coach training program almost immediately following the experience. As a high-level influencer in his company, Gene continually shared with others about coaching and was able to generate interest and commitment from his CEO to launch a coaching climate. Today, several years later, Gene continues to be an advocate for coaching, an attitude that has spread throughout his company.

Before launching a corporate coaching climate, it's important to be clear about the purpose of the coaching. Stating clear objectives, usually related to the development of others, helps link coaching with the organization's strategic objectives and needs. In one utility company, coaching is linked directly with the need for succession planning and top talent development and retention. In other companies, it is linked to the organization's "climate survey," a measure of employee satisfaction.

High-level leaders who are proponents of coaching need to be sure that the initiative links with strategic objectives, becomes a leadership competency, and is positioned as a way of focusing on organizational needs in the future. To that end, they should consider the following questions when planning to launch a coaching culture:

- What is our definition of coaching?
- What makes it so important to our business?
- What results do we expect by using coaching in the organization?
- Who will be the senior leadership stakeholders for strategy and high-level linkages?
- What inspiring stories can our internal champions share with others?
- How will the stories be shared?
- What is our message about coaching?
- Who will our coaches be? Will we use coaches who are internal, external, leaders/managers, or a combination?
- Where will coaching reside, and who will have oversight of the coaches?
- Who will get coaching?
- What kinds of coaching will be offered?
- What outcomes/deliverables will be expected of coaching?
- How will we track and measure the effectiveness of coaching?

Making It Real

- Who are your high-level internal sponsors?
- How do you see coaching linked to your organization's strategic objectives?

IDENTIFYING INTERNAL CHAMPIONS FOR IMPLEMENTATION

In addition to leadership stakeholders who share the vision of coaching, it is critical to have internal champions. Internal champions may be individuals who are charged with doing internal coaching or who oversee coaching. These people are involved with coaching at an implementation level, and as they develop others and meet organizational goals, they show by their daily interactions that coaching really works.

In one pharmaceutical company, Val, a senior leader, learned about coaching but couldn't get approval for formal training. Although her company wouldn't pay for it, she enrolled in a coach training program on her own. And, more importantly, without telling anyone what she was doing, she started coaching her team.

Informally, Val created a coaching climate with her direct reports, and they started to meet or exceed all their deliverables. This caught the attention of the VP and, ultimately, the CEO of the company, who asked what was happening within Val's group. The leaders talked to each person on the team, who verified that Val's leadership made the difference. Val shared that the only thing she was doing differently was to use coaching competencies in all appropriate interactions. As a result of finding this pocket of coaching, other areas of the organization embraced coaching. Val moved out of her current role and began to work as an internal coach. Eventually, she took on the responsibility for hiring, training, and overseeing other internal coaches, and became an internal champion for coaching in her organization. Today, Val's company encourages and embraces a coaching climate.

WHERE COACHING RESIDES

Part of the challenge for organizations creating a coaching climate is determining where coaching resides. In some organizations, coaching is located in the human resources (HR) or organizational development (OD) department. For other organizations, it is part of leadership development or a corporate university.

Once it has been determined where coaching resides, people can be selected as the internal champions to develop the strategy and implementation. Some people will naturally gravitate toward coaching. Others won't. Be sure those who become internal champions have the passion, desire, and entrepreneurial spirit to launch and expand the reach of coaching.

As coaching spreads, some people will want to get involved as internal coaches or as facilitators, if coach training programs are offered. The key is to be certain that the right people are selected to help launch coaching, especially early in the process.

The right people:

- are usually collaborative by nature.
- see others as capable and creative, trusting them to solve problems and make decisions.
- share feedback in a timely way and ask for feedback on their own behavior and impact.
- want the best not only for themselves but also for the organization and team members.
- are focused on developing others, as well as on projects and goals.
- are gracious when mistakes are made and look for the learning in them.
- model coaching in all interactions.

Making It Real

- Who comes to mind when you think about the qualities of internal coaches?
- How can they become engaged with future coaching?
- What other qualities come to mind as you think about internal coaches in your organization?

TRAINING INTERNAL COACHES

Once the right people have been identified to help create a coaching climate, they need to be trained as coaches. Many coach training opportunities are available. One of the best resources for a list of schools is the International Coach Federation (ICF; www.CoachFederation.org), which accredits coach training programs and certifies individual coaches. Training is an ideal starting point for acquiring the skills and competencies of a coach.

While many schools are accredited by the ICF, few are solely focused on coaching inside organizations. The purpose of training for internal coaches is to teach how coaching can be used effectively inside an organization, which is different from training to help people become professional external coaches. Be careful to look for coach training programs that are suited to organizational coaching.

If a large number of people from the organization are being trained in coaching, there are a variety of ways to get started. One organization with 20 coaches decided to have its coaches go through two different training programs so they could share what they'd learned with each other. During and after their training, they met regularly to share their experiences, similarities, and differences. Another company with more than 100 internal coaches used one coach training school predominantly. That company has a consistent language surrounding coaching that has served them well. Other companies don't specify which schools to attend. Instead, they leave it up to the individuals to select the coach training program.

Being coached is another way to learn about coaching. Every coach training school has professional coaches leading classes and modeling coaching, and most schools recommend that participants experience coaching first-hand. Working with a professional coach who can serve as both a coach and a mentor helps to jump-start the learning process. Working with a number of coaches offers a broad perspective on what coaching is and how to employ it most effectively.

Equally important in learning about coaching is getting as much experience as soon as possible coaching others. The late Thomas Leonard, widely recognized as a pioneer in the field of coaching, would tell his students: "You aren't really a coach until you've coached at least 100 people." He was referring to the learning that occurs for the coach while coaching others. Even in the early stages of coaching, it is acceptable to coach others and to start practicing as soon as possible in order to learn from each coaching interaction. Internal coaches should be instructed to keep a log that includes the following:

- Coach training hours
- Contact information and hours spent coaching others
- Contact information and hours they are coached by a certified coach
- Key learnings from each coaching interaction

For more guidelines, go to the ICF Web site, at www.coach federation.org.

IMPLEMENTING INTERNAL COACHING

If your organization is planning to implement internal coaching, there are a number of questions that are best answered early in the planning stages. The questions in Table 2.1 are intended to serve as a starting place, not an exhaustive list. They can also serve as the basis for internal communications about coaching, for those who are coaching as well as those receiving coaching.

DEVELOPING A SYSTEMATIC APPROACH TO INTERNAL COACHING

Getting trained as a coach and practicing with others are starting points when creating an internal coaching climate. If there is a

Table 2.1

Coaching Questions to Aid Implementation

Questions for Internal Coaches	Information Needed by People Being Coached
What is the business reason for using internal versus external coaches?	Who is eligible for coaching? How are people who are eligible for coaching informed that it is available to them?
What are the specific objectives for coaching?	
How will the organization know if the coaching has been successful?	
How are internal coaches chosen?	
What criteria are used to screen them?	
To whom do coaches report?	
Is coaching part of or exclusively the coaches' role?	
Who is responsible for ongoing oversight, training, and development of internal coaches?	What is the process for matching coaches with those being coached?
What is the coaching methodology?	What is the process for orienting people to coaching?
What content is used for training and orientation of people being coached?	What is the process for connecting people with their coaches?
What is the process for training and orientation of internal coaches?	
What kinds of coaching are offered? (This refers to leadership development coaching, coaching to support learning, performance coaching, etc.)	How much coaching do people receive, and how frequently are they coached?

(Continued)

Table 2.1

Coaching Questions to Aid Implementation (*Continued*)

Questions for Internal Coaches	Information Needed by People Being Coached
How will coaches connect with their clients?	How can people extend their coaching if they want more?
What information will coaches receive about their clients?	What is the recourse for a person who finds the coaching is
How will coaches schedule and deliver coaching?	unsatisfactory?
Will managers be included in the coaching process?	What is communicated about the
If not, what information will they get about the coaching?	coaching, to whom and by whom?
If so, how will communication with managers be managed?	What will be expected of people being coached in terms of communication about their coaching?
What record-keeping and documentation will be expected of the coaches, such as sessions completed, information about what is happening in the sessions, and so forth?	How is success measured and communicated with others?
What process will coaches use to share information with appropriate parties?	

desire to have internal coaches, an infrastructure to support the coaching should be built.

It is beyond the scope of this book to lay out a comprehensive systematic approach, as each organization is unique. Thus, the infrastructure and approach will have to be customized to meet the specific needs and objectives for each coaching environment. Nevertheless, there are a number of questions to consider, the answers to which can serve as guidelines for developing an appropriate approach.

WHAT IS YOUR DEFINITION OF COACHING?

A first step is to define coaching for your organization. As noted in Chapter 1, definitions of coaching abound. Whether your organization develops its own definition or uses one from a different source, be sure it is specifically related to the organization's desired outcomes. For example, one organization defines coaching simply as "facilitating the development of others." Another defines it as "a specific process by which individuals are developed for sustained improvement and business results." Having a definition for coaching helps to paint a picture for others about what the process will mean within the organization.

WHAT IS YOUR INTERNAL COMMUNICATION PLAN?

To expand coaching inside an organization, a strategic internal communication plan should be developed. Think about who needs to know about coaching, what they need to know, when they need to know it, and how the information will be communicated. The communication plan might include the following:

- Sending multiple short messages through an internal newsletter.
- Scheduling key leaders to leave voice messages on a regular basis.
- Sending well-planned emails that contain pertinent information.

In one organization, people who had been coached gave permission to share their experiences in internal communications.

Making It Real

As an internal communications plan is being established, think about:

- What are the intended benefits of the coaching?
- How do the benefits link to the overall initiatives and corporate strategy?
- Who are the sponsors at strategic and implementation levels?
- What can people expect when they are coached?
- What are the timelines for rollout?

WHO WILL BE DOING THE COACHING?

A key question to ask and answer about internal coaching climates is, "Who will do the coaching?" Is it the manager's job? Are there designated internal coaches? Will external coaches be used at certain levels? All of the above?

Any coach, internal or external, should be able to adequately answer the questions in Table 2.2 prior to starting the coaching engagement, in order to avoid ugly surprises. Even coaches who have experience with the company as a whole will want to familiarize themselves with the special political climate, confidentiality strictures, specific culture, and other distinctions particular to the area they are working in and the objectives of the engagement.

In some organizations, managers are expected to use coaching skills as part of their roles. If so, they need to be trained to understand exactly what coaching means and how to do it. In other organizations, internal coaches, often as part of the HR function, have coaching as part of their job descriptions. This needs to be clearly articulated in any communications that go out. Still other companies use a combination of internal and external coaches,

Table 2.2

Coach Checklist

Number	Questions	√	Answers/Notes
Politics			
1	What is the political power structure of this organization?		
2	Who is your sponsor in the organization, and what are that person's goals?		
3	Does your organizational contact have the respect of others?		
4	Does your organizational contact have authority?		
5	Who in the organization disagrees with the decision to initiate a coaching program?		
6	What are the goals of these people?		
7	How might these people be influenced?		
8	Is there any way the coaching program might be undermined or sabotaged, inadvertently or not?		
Confidentiality			
1	When you're hired by an organization to work with one or more individuals, who is the client?		
2	How will you communicate about confidentiality with your sponsor and with individuals being coached?		

(*Continued*)

Table 2.2

Coach Checklist (*Continued*)

Number	Questions	√	Answers/Notes
3	With whom do you share information, and what is the nature of that information? (Legalities must also be considered. For example, what must be reported by law, such as crimes? To whom and when must it be reported?)		
4	What themes and patterns related to the initiatives can be shared with management?		
5	Is your written contract clear regarding confidentiality?		
6	How do you best establish a confidential relationship with the individuals you're coaching?		
7	What do you do when the organizational contact asks you for information about the individuals being coached?		
8	How will you get buy-in from the individuals being coached if the organization has hired you?		
9	How much support will you get from the organization to support education, enrollment, and feedback?		
10	Are there any potential confidentiality pitfalls within this organization that you can be aware of now?		

Table 2.2

Coach Checklist (*Continued*)

Number	Questions	√	Answers/Notes
Culture			
1	How will you familiarize yourself with the language, norms, and protocols of the organization?		
2	Can you identify any underlying cultural trends or expectations in this organization?		
3	How do people treat each other in the organization? (Is the person/relationship more important than the result/deliverable, or vice versa?)		
4	How are birthdays, births, illnesses, and other personal events/situations treated?		
5	How is physical space used? (Is it shared or defended? Is there a communal feeling or territorial attitude?)		
6	How do people in the culture identify themselves? (Is individuality encouraged or discouraged? Do employees dress in a uniform way?)		
7	How do people treat time? (Is there a "work-harder-than-thou" competitive quality? Do people leave at a reasonable hour in full view of their colleagues, or do they slip out leaving a jacket behind and the lights on?)		

(*Continued*)

Table 2.2

Coach Checklist (*Continued*)

Number	Questions	✓	Answers/Notes
8	How do people communicate and exchange information? (Is email the accepted form of communication, or do employees rely on conversation?)		
9	How many remote workers are there? How does this affect in-house employees? How does this affect your work?		
10	What is the observable balance of business results versus value on people?		
Coaching versus Consulting			
1	What language do you use to distinguish coaching from consulting, particularly when establishing a coaching relationship with the organization and with the individuals being coached?		
2	Precisely, how do you offer a coach approach when you have areas of expertise from which the organization or individuals being coached might benefit?		
3	In what ways do you add value other than offering expertise?		
4	Do you foresee a need in this organization for consulting, as opposed to coaching? In what areas?		

Table 2.2

Coach Checklist (*Continued*)

Number	Questions	√	Answers/Notes
5	How will you meet the consulting need? How will you handle necessary referrals for issues you might encounter with individuals being coached, such as need for therapy, addiction counseling, and so forth?		
6	Do you have professional consulting resources available for use on this project, if necessary?		
7	Is any of your expertise in the area(s) where this organization may need consulting? If so, how will you handle this potential dilemma?		
8	How will you clarify to both the organization and the people being coached that your role is as coach, not consultant?		
9	How can you become more comfortable being only coach, and not slipping into the consultant role?		
10	How will you prevent the individuals being coached and the organization from falling into the habit of using you as a consultant?		

(*Continued*)

Table 2.2

Coach Checklist (*Continued*)

Number	Questions	√	Answers/Notes
Tracking and Accounting			
1	Are you a detail person, capable of providing the kind of tracking necessary for this engagement?		
2	What kind of internal administrative help will you be offered?		
3	Will you have resources and staff available to use in the administrative and tracking mode for this project? (Should you be building in fees for this service, regardless of what help you are promised?)		
4	Have you delineated the administrative, tracking, and accounting requirements for this engagement?		
5	How will individuals sign up for coaching, and how will communication be handled?		
6	Who will schedule appointments, and how will rescheduling be handled?		
7	What is the cancellation policy?		
8	If you are on-site, who will book the space you require?		
9	What are the communication protocols within this organization, for you, the individuals being coached, and management?		

Table 2.2

Coach Checklist (*Continued*)

Number	Questions	√	Answers/Notes
10	What are invoicing specifics?		
Triangles			
1	Do you have definition, clear language, and understanding of triangles? How will you communicate this concept to both the organization and those being coached?		
2	What communication issues need to be considered at the onset of this contractual agreement?		
3	How will you set up your contract initially to prevent triangles?		
4	How will "who brought you in" versus "who you are working with" affect the engagement?		
5	How can you start coaching quickly and strongly so that individuals being coached feel they can trust you?		
6	To whom have you communicated what information will be shared, with whom and by whom?		
7	To whom do you actually report, and how will you disseminate information to this person?		
8	How will ongoing communication happen to prevent triangles?		

(*Continued*)

Table 2.2

Coach Checklist (*Continued*)

Number	Questions	√	Answers/Notes
9	Who has what power in the relationship, and who is acting out?		
10	How can you help both the organization and those being coached gain clarity about triangles and potential triangle situations?		

Measurement and Evaluation

Number	Questions	√	Answers/Notes
1	How will you and the organization know what to measure, and how will you define success?		
2	How can you know that you are clear as to why you are coaching in the organization?		
3	How has your presence been communicated to individuals being coached?		
4	Have all deliverables been contracted, up front and in writing?		
5	What expertise can be shared or brought in to help the organization measure the effectiveness of the coaching initiative?		
6	What surveys or assessments will you (or others) perform up front and measure against at the end?		

Table 2.2
Coach Checklist (*Continued*)

Number	Questions	✓	Answers/Notes
7	How will you measure data without skewing it?		
8	How will you use the data to show whether or not the coaching was worth the investment? What if it wasn't? How will you handle that?		
9	Would your organization be content with qualitative, anecdotal feedback from individual participants? If so, are there any parameters for this feedback?		
10	What is required to collect this anecdotal feedback and deliver it to the organization?		
Personal			
1	What specifically, do you need right now to be ready for this coaching engagement? (Do you need, for example, additional training or particular resources?)		
2	Where is your personal development in terms of this coaching engagement?		
3	What plan will you put into place to move forward in your personal development, in general, and as it relates to this engagement?		

(*Continued*)

Table 2.2

Coach Checklist (*Continued*)

Number	Questions	√	Answers/Notes
4	Do you have any beliefs or attitudes about organizations (or about this organization in particular) that may interfere with your coaching?		
5	How can you anticipate preconceived attitudes and make plans to prevent them from interfering?		
6	Do you have clearly defined values, and are you prepared to stand up for them in this organization?		
7	Are you going into this engagement completely confident in your abilities as a coach and competent businessperson?		
8	Are there any personal issues that you need to address regarding this engagement that may have been missed?		
9	If you are working as a solo coach in this engagement, how might you plan to add other coaches, if necessary, for any contract expansion? What will be your criteria?		
10	Have you determined up front, prior to this engagement, that you will always take the "high road," claim responsibility, and act with integrity throughout the project?		

knowing that some executives prefer to work with an external coach to enable increased confidentiality, objectivity, and honest input.

WHAT TYPES OF COACHING WILL BE OFFERED?

Many types of coaching are used in organizations. Determining the most appropriate for your company must be based on what it most needs. For example:

- Do employees attend training but then fail to apply the information in practice? If so, then coaching to support learning may be appropriate.
- Do key leaders or employees with high potential need to be able to move into new positions more efficiently? If so, then leadership development coaching may be the best fit.
- Is the industry shifting in ways that require organizational strategy and executive-level changes?
- Is there a need for a clear succession strategy? If so, then executive coaching should be considered.
- Are there valuable key leaders in your organization who have performance issues that need to be addressed? If so, then performance coaching may be the answer.

The point is, be sure to take the time to determine which offerings are most relevant to achieve the desired business results.

WHAT'S THE PROCESS FOR PEOPLE WHO WANT TO BE COACHED?

It's Friday morning. Alex has had a rough week with his team on a project that has a tight deadline. The team is not working well together. Alex feels as if he's had to baby-sit all week, and he's ready to fire the entire team. On Wednesday, Alex spoke with his manager about these challenges. During their conversation, Alex became aware that he was contributing to the turmoil and that his leadership skills needed improvement. As his manager asked revealing questions, Alex began to think of other ways to work with his team.

Because Alex was so open and eager to improve his skills, his manager suggested that Alex might benefit from additional coaching, and explained that there were internal coaches who might be helpful. Alex was intrigued and asked how to get started.

Organizations need a process for those people who want formal coaching from an internal coach. Informal coaching can happen at any time. Setting up a formal coaching structure requires thought and intentional action. One of the first questions to be answered is: "Who is eligible for coaching?" Executives only? Executives and managers? Anyone with supervisory responsibility? Again, since each organization is different, this question begs a strategic discussion based on what is going on and what the organizational needs are.

Assuming that there are internal coaches as part of the coaching climate, it is important to clarify how people sign up for coaching. Is it a self-selection process? Do individuals, such as Alex, need to be recommended for coaching by a manager? May others nominate someone for coaching? These questions need to be answered so that systems can be created to support the decisions made.

WHAT DOCUMENTATION IS NEEDED?

Anticipating and developing the systems and documentation, before the coaching launch, helps people know what to expect from the coaching process. Knowing who is responsible for the coaching, and who to talk to if something goes awry, offers reassurance and security when challenges arise.

When building an internal coaching climate, documentation can be extremely useful. Most often, documentation includes downloadable or printable material in the form of manuals or handbooks that cover information both for the coaches and the people being coached. Having this information readily accessible to the people who need it is vital. This includes managers who might be recommending people to be coached, coaches, and the individuals who will receive coaching.

In addition, think about the process for signing up. Will you provide a formal registration form? Or will an informal email or voice mail sign-up be sufficient? Who will oversee the coaching, to ensure that the best coach is working with each individual? What is the monitoring process for the coaching?

NOTE

See the Sample Coaching Participant Manual in Appendix I.

An organization with 5,000 employees has 10 designated internal coaches. Bernie, the company champion who helped launch internal coaching, oversees these coaches. On Wednesday, when Bernie arrived at his office, he found coaching requests from seven people. Five of the requests came via email and voice mail, with general information about the people wanting coaching. Two of the requests came via the form provided on the company's intranet, which asks for name, job title, manager's name, reason for requesting coaching, contact, and other pertinent information.

Bernie sighed deeply as he listened to the voice messages and read the emails that had bypassed the intranet system. But he smiled when he saw the two intranet-generated forms waiting for him. As he looked through them, specific coaches came to mind who would be good for each of the people who had requested coaching. He knew the capacity of each internal coach and made assignments based on that knowledge. He then used an email template to respond to the people being coached, as well as to the coaches who would be assigned to work with them. He smiled again, realizing how helpful the template was. Having all the information—the name of the person being coached, the coach, the number of coaching sessions, how coaching would take place (in this case, by telephone), what would be reported and to whom, and general information about what to expect—had made his task so much easier. He hit the Send button and leaned back in his chair.

But, not for long, for Bernie then had to email the five people who had contacted him directly, instead of completing the online form. He sent each one an email with a link to the document that needed to be filled out. Again, he sighed, wondering when everyone would use the appropriate systems and processes he had created for everyone's convenience. Next, he scheduled a meeting for all the internal coaches to discuss what they were learning about coaching and how to expand it in their company. And then he. . . .

Just what does Bernie have to do with creating a coaching climate? All of the tasks that Bernie was dealing with are those that need to be addressed when setting up internal coaching. Thinking through the many questions and implications helps establish a strong system of internal coaching. In addition, flexibility and adaptability are vital to the ebb and flow of coaching. As input is received from people who are being coached and from the coaches, refinements to the process or systems can be made. The key is to learn from every experience of coaching.

CHALLENGES THAT ARISE WITH COACHING

Whenever there are external or internal coaches involved in organizations, challenges will arise. They may take the form of failing to have the right systems in place, or not in a timely fashion. Challenges may come in matching the right coach with the person being coached. Or they may come from the myriad surprises that inevitably occur when people work together.

It is wise to expect challenges, and to know who the primary contact is to address them. This means that if someone doesn't like what is going on in coaching, he or she knows with whom to speak internally. Or if someone needs a different level coach, that individual knows where to turn. For the coaches, it means that if there's a challenge with a person they're coaching, they have a safe and confidential colleague to discuss the problem with, and together, they can determine next steps and appropriate actions.

As coaching is launched, and gains momentum within the organization, it's a good idea to share success stories, as they can be inspiring and help engage others in a coaching process. Be sure that before publicizing successes, permission has been granted to include personal and department names. If not, publicize the stories anonymously. Confidentiality is critical to the success of coaching, so when someone requests anonymity, respect the request.

MEASURING THE SUCCESS OF INTERNAL COACHING

With any kind of organizational coaching, it's important to know up front what success looks like and how it will be measured. When establishing the strategy for internal coaching, have clear objectives. For example, one objective may be to prepare key leaders for their next positions. Most organizations already know the average length of time, usually months or years, it takes before new leaders find their stride. If this is one of the objectives, measure how much more quickly this has occurred as a result of coaching.

NOTE

See Chapter 5 for expanded coverage of this topic.

One objective may have to do with the churn rate, and the need to increase retention of sales reps. Most organizations already know what the current churn is and how much it costs. If this is an objective, encourage a number of sales leaders to be coached and then measure their increased retention against those who aren't getting coached.

A second objective may be to help a key leader learn how to influence direct reports differently. Evaluation for this objective may include interviews, surveys, 360-degree feedback, or just "word on the street" input. If this is the objective, consider making coaching available to the people on the leader's team so that they can learn how to work more effectively with the leader, too.

Many companies are beginning to reap the benefits of using coaching in a strategic way. These companies are seeing their corporate cultures change. But make no mistake: creating a coaching climate isn't a quick fix. It takes several years to shift a culture.

Driving cultural change, including coaching, takes relentless focus, patience, and persistence. It takes a clear strategy linked to organizational objectives, in conjunction with buy-in from the top. It can be done, and it's worth it.

Making It Real

- Where is your organization in its readiness for a coaching climate?
- In what specific ways can you influence others toward coaching?
- In what specific areas do you need to develop, personally and within your organization, to model a coaching approach?

The Nonnegotiables

Certain nonnegotiables must be in place before an organization offers coaching. These are explored in the following subsections.

When Valerie, an HR professional in the aerospace industry, was tasked with looking into how coaching could benefit her company, she knew she needed help. As she began to look around, she discovered a plethora of information from many vantage points. Continuing to explore, Valerie identified a number of themes inherent in coaching, regardless of who she talked to. She soon correctly decided that, in order for coaching to be effective in her company, she would need to insist that certain nonnegotiables be a part of the coaching initiative.

Valerie was a smart woman! As she learned about coaching, she recognized that many people offer professional coaching, some of whom are excellent, very effective coaches who know how to create strong, healthy coaching relationships. To create the relationships that foster effective organizational coaching, certain nonnegotiables must be in place. These include:

- Senior level buy-in (executive support)
- Clearly stated WIIFM (what's in it for me)—clear identification of professional and corporate benefits
- Confidentiality in coaching relationships
- Action
- Internal marketing
- Excellent administration

Senior-Level Buy-in

Top-level support is critical for coaching and other leadership development efforts to be successful, says Scott Blanchard, vice president of delivery with The Ken Blanchard Companies. Senior-level buy-in comes as people learn about coaching and share resources and experiences about it. Microsoft offers regular and frequent *webinars* (Web-based seminars), including those with a focus on coaching. Many books and articles discuss coaching and its benefits. The *Harvard Business Review, Fast Company*, and *Wall Street Journal* are just a few publications that regularly publish information about coaching.

When leaders personally engage in the process of coaching, they are modeling the level of involvement they want from others. Even if executive leaders don't participate personally in the coaching process, they must clearly endorse and be committed to the benefits of coaching. The more connections made from executive levels in the organization, the better the enrollment and engagement by individuals receiving coaching.

In one high-tech company where a large number of people were being coached, the entire executive team was required to participate in an on-site launch of the coaching initiative. The purpose of having them present for the launch was to acknowledge the importance of the coaching and the sponsorship by top-level leadership. As part of the meeting, several executives shared their own experiences being coached. Needless to say, there was almost 100 percent enrollment and completion of the coaching process.

Clearly Stated WIIFM

How often do you have to take precious time away from your work to do something you aren't sure will be beneficial? How motivated would you be to participate in something you didn't think was relevant? How many meetings do you attend each week that fit those criteria?

For coaching to be embraced universally, it must be linked to company objectives. Coaching can support strategic initiatives, develop "bench strength," encourage professional development, and leverage training time and dollars. Whatever the purpose of the coaching initiative in your company, be sure to link it strategically to the organization's goals and objectives, as well as to the individual's role in the company.

When the coaching initiative was rolled out at a manufacturing company, the division VP sent several emails to explain why coaching was being used to develop leaders. One leader, Ken, was resistant to being coached. Maybe he was too busy to read the memos sent by his VP, or he didn't realize how important it was. He may not have recognized that coaching was a way to develop future leaders, or thought that others needed it, but not him. He may even have thought that he was too important for that warm-and-fuzzy stuff called coaching. Unfortunately, when Ken's VP heard that Ken wasn't engaged yet with his coach, she was upset. She decided that even though it would take valuable time, it was important to let him know, in no uncertain terms, what was expected of him in this regard.

"Ken, we know that you haven't participated in the coaching initiative yet," she began. "But this is part of the process for our future leaders, and if you want to continue to rise through the ranks, we suggest you be in touch with your coach, ASAP! Coaching is part of our leadership development process. We expect you to be on board with it."

As soon as Ken understood that his participation in his company's coaching initiative would be linked to his potential future promotions in the company, he embraced the initiative.

Making It Real

Coaching can be effective in a number of ways. Answer the following questions to clearly identify personal and corporate benefits to coaching:

- On a scale of 1 to 10, how engaged are you at work? What would help you to be more so?
- How clear are you on your key responsibility areas? What would increase your clarity if needed?
- What goals do you have that would benefit from coaching?
- What have you been thinking about but not taking action on that could help your team/organization?
- How would increased collaboration help you in accomplishing your goals?
- How would giving timely feedback improve the performance of others?
- What would be different if you had time to think strategically on a regular basis?

Confidentiality in Coaching Relationships

Wherever coaching exists in organizations, it is critical to clearly articulate what confidentiality means. Confidentiality needs to be addressed differently when external coaches are involved versus when the coaching is housed within the organization.

When an organization decides to use external coaches, confidentiality occurs at two discreet levels. The first level is with the organization as the client. The second level is with the individuals being coached.

At the first level of confidentiality, with the organization, a good working relationship must be established between the external coach(es) and the internal sponsor who oversees the coaching initiative. Often, when teams of external coaches are involved, a head coach oversees the coaching. Prior to getting started, the head coach (or the external coach) and the internal sponsor determine what will and will not be shared about the coaching. The head coach works closely with the coaches and with the organizational sponsor, communicating frequently with both to ensure successful coaching while maintaining confidentiality. Normally, the head coach does not have direct contact with the individuals being coached but rather with the organizational sponsor.

At the second level of confidentiality, with the individuals being coached, the organizational sponsor has direct contact with the people being coached and their managers. The individual coaches also have direct contact with the individuals being coached. Confidentiality is required at this level. As depicted in Figure 2.1, setting up the structure in this way encourages increased communication and feedback within the organization, rather than relying on the coaching team for feedback.

With internal coaches, the dynamics are slightly different. The internal sponsor with oversight responsibility is in direct contact with the coaches. The sponsor must also be in contact with the individuals being coached to communicate what to expect, to share who the coach will be, and to serve as the liaison if there is a challenge. As depicted in Figure 2.2, the internal sponsor may be in some communication with the managers, but only in setting up the coaching initiative. The person being coached is responsible for keeping his or her manager updated on what is happening with coaching.

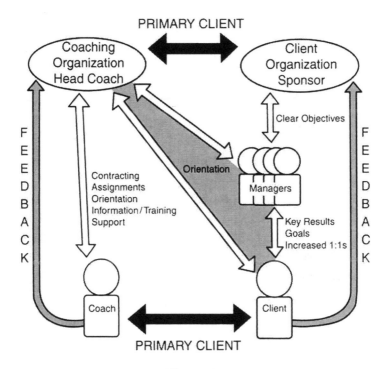

Figure 2.1
Confidentiality with External Coaching

In most organizations, confidentiality means that the coach, whether internal or external, will not share with anyone what is being discussed during the sessions. In other organizations, it means that the coach does not share content with the person's manager or with the HR professional involved. Whatever the definition of confidentiality in an organization, it must be clearly spelled out and adhered to in order for safe, open coaching relationships to exist.

All coaching must include clear agreements around confidentiality on three discrete levels:

- *Confidentiality within the company.* When companies are spending money on coaching, regardless of whether the coaches are internal or external, confidentiality within the

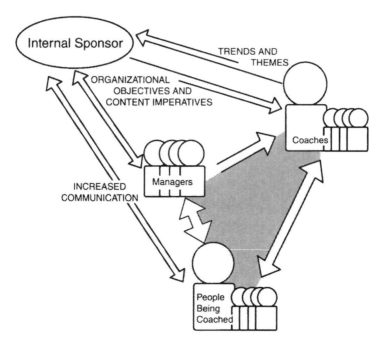

Figure 2.2
Confidentiality with Internal Coaching

company must be considered. Some companies want their HR professionals or internal sponsors to know what is happening within the coaching relationship. This needs to be discussed as part of all coaching agreements. The effective coach expects clear agreements, often in writing, about what is shared and with whom. It is normal to expect that the number of sessions and the level of engagement may be discussed, but not the content of the coaching sessions. In some cases, trends or themes can be reported back to the company, described carefully to protect individual content.

- *Confidentiality with the person being coached.* This, also, is critical for internal or external coaches. Again, establishing clear agreements about what communications will occur, how frequently, and with whom helps create a safe environment in which the coaching will take place.

- *Confidentiality about what is shared by the coach regarding trade secrets.* Effective coaches state clearly and up front that they will not pass anything on to others inside or outside of the coaching relationship. This includes not sharing anything relating to organizational charts or any other strategic or tactical information.

One way to express confidentiality is as follows:

"Everything within the coaching relationship stays within the coaching relationship. Coaches will not disclose any content being discussed. Coaches may be asked to share the number of sessions completed and how engaged clients seem to be. In those instances only, coaches will share information. If clients want to talk about the content of the coaching sessions, they are free to do so. The coaches will not."

Along with this approach, an effective coach encourages clients to increase communication with key stakeholders, including managers, HR professionals, team members, and colleagues. In this way, coaching can increase communication when the coach encourages the person being coached to share directly with those who need to be included.

Action

Coaching is about action—effective, intentional action. Whether the action is to think about something or to do something, action is an explicit part of coaching. Taking action just for the sake of taking action is, however, nothing more than a form of busy-ness, which is not what coaching is about.

When coaching inside organizations, actions need to be aligned with the individual's key responsibility areas, along with team and organizational goals. Actions that may emerge from coaching include taking specific next steps, committing to something that's been explicitly discussed, discussing a situation with someone by a certain date, or thinking about a specific strategy or challenge.

Some people are not ready for coaching because they are not ready or willing to take action. But that doesn't mean that there's a problem with the person. Sometimes the timing may be wrong, due to commitments or other projects that are in the works. If that is the case, coaching should be delayed or offered to others who are better positioned to move ahead.

Internal Marketing

An internal marketing plan is vital if coaching is to be respected and encouraged in organizations. The plan works best if it includes clear statements about: what coaching is (and is not), who will be doing the coaching (external coaches or internal, or both), how it is positioned, who is eligible, who the senior-level champions are, who the go-to person is, how confidentiality will be handled, how to get started, coaching parameters (how many sessions, method—by phone or face to face, how to extend the coaching, etc.), how managers fit in, and how it will be measured. All of these must be addressed in the context of the specific goals and objectives of the organization.

Excellent Administration

One challenge with coaching within organizations is how to manage it. Putting systems in place to set up and track the coaching process is critical. Many organizations don't realize how challenging this can be!

NOTE

See Chapter 4 for more on measuring the success of coaching.

An initial question to ask is: Who "owns" the coaching. HR? OD? The leadership and development function? Regardless of the area it resides in, who there specifically owns it? All of these must be determined up front, with senior-level support.

Once the question is answered about where coaching resides, it's time to decide how to enroll people in coaching; how to match coaches with internal clients; how to bring closure or respond to requests for extended coaching; and how to track, report, and measure success. There are no cookie-cutter answers to any of these questions, as each organization is unique. What is absolutely imperative is having more administrative support than you think you will need!

Taking Action

- Which areas are already strong and which need to be strengthened if your organization is to implement coaching successfully?
- What knowledge or experience do you have with effective coaching in other organizations that you can bring into your organization?
- What else do you need to know about coaching in order to be well informed?

CHAPTER 3

Managing the Coaching Experience

EVERY COACHING EXPERIENCE should be a journey with a clear and definable destination, and the coach is responsible for managing the pathways. If a person being coached walks away from a coaching conversation thinking, "Well, that felt good, but I am not sure what I really accomplished," then the coach is not paying enough attention to managing the coaching experience.

One major predictor of coaching success is how much attention is given to setting up the coaching partnership. A coaching partnership, like any relationship, flourishes when clear agreements exist up front. In addition, the coaching experience will only be successful if the goals for coaching are laid out up front and the milestones are tracked diligently. Finally, much growth in coaching can be subtle, with results that will only be realized over time, so the person being coached should be made aware of what is being accomplished throughout the course of coaching.

STARTING ON THE RIGHT FOOT

Ken Blanchard has said that when you take care of the beginning, the end takes care of itself. This is absolutely true of coaching. The following measures will ensure a productive coaching relationship and create a nurturing environment for the person being coached:

CONTRACTING

The person being coached should have a clear understanding of:

- What coaching is.
- What it isn't.
- What is expected of the coach.
- What is expected of the person being coached.
- What the person being coached might expect to accomplish with coaching.
- What is and what is not held in confidence. Of course, the more confidentiality is assured, the more candid a person being coached will be. However, if a coach is paid by an organization, he or she will be expected to share a certain amount of information. At the minimum, the organization will want to know if and when the coaching started and how many coaching sessions have occurred. Ideally, the person being coached will be encouraged to share some details about the coaching experience with his or her manager or coaching sponsor and will be given some sort of communication tool to do this. In addition, the person being coached must be informed, up front, what kinds of issues the coach is obligated (as an agent of the organization) to report if they come up in coaching, such as allegations of fraud, discrimination, or harassment.
- Organizational contact if the person being coached is not comfortable with the coach and is not able to effect a change by giving the coach feedback.

The coach and person being coached must establish together:

- What a good coaching experience looks like for the person being coached. The coach can ask the person being coached when in the past someone has been helpful, and extrapolate from past successes what kind of style might work best.

- How the coaching will take place, including frequency, form (on the phone or face to face), additional email/voice mail contact between coaching conversations.
- Duration of the coaching contract.
- Vision for the coaching. The vision can be established by answering the question: "What is the best-case scenario if the coaching is successful?"
- Goals for coaching. Goals can be established by answering the question: "What will be different at the end of the coaching engagement?"
- Goals may be used to establish clear focus areas and to craft an action plan. Alternatively, the person being coached will have input from his or her manager about development needs, or may have a good idea based on personal observations. The person being coached may give permission to the coach to interview stakeholders, such as colleagues and direct reports, to get input about strengths to leverage and areas for development or attention. Individuals are often surprisingly aware of their development needs and are eager to discuss them in a safe environment.

COACHABILITY QUESTIONS

A coach might use the following questions to assess whether someone is a good fit for coaching. In general, the coach is looking for ability, readiness, and willingness to be coached.

Is the person who wants to be coached:

- Planning to stay in his or her role and/or grow with the organization for at least the next six months?
- Currently feeling successful in his or her role and the organization?
- On an even keel from a performance standpoint (may have some challenges, but no serious problems)?
- Eager to obtain, consider, and be influenced by feedback?

- Familiar with coaching or open to learning about coaching?
- Open to new perspectives?
- Experienced at learning from others?
- Able to devote at least one hour or more per week to coaching sessions or commitments made in coaching sessions?
- Willing to be challenged?
- Self-confident enough to disagree with the coach and/or to give the coach feedback if coaching doesn't feel useful?
- Able to do some introspection?
- Eager to grow and change?
- On an even keel personally; not grappling with severe personal problems that currently require focus, such as addiction recovery, grief, difficult relationship issues that require close attention/therapy/counseling, contentious divorce/custody/legal issues?

The coach will have to assess whether coaching is the best way to serve the person who is potentially to be coached. Often, the decision is an intuitive one, but this checklist can help the coach pinpoint the specific set of circumstances that will help determine whether the person is a good coaching candidate. If the individual is not, the coach can express his or her reservation and gauge the person's response. In addition, the coach may recommend other service providers (financial planner, therapist, addiction counselor) to work with the person instead of, or in addition to, the coaching. The key is that the coach has to have the courage and integrity to point out when coaching isn't right and be willing to give up a client.

COACHING SESSION PREPARATION FORM FOR PERSON BEING COACHED

The coach may want to encourage the person being coached to prepare for each coaching session by looking at the past, present, and future in regard to the coaching relationship. Such preparation helps focus the thoughts of the person being coached,

---

Ideal Coaching Participant Profile

In setting up an organizational coaching initiative, the following profile may be helpful in selecting participants. Ideal coaching participants are

- Enthusiastic about the concept of continuous professional development and learning
- Willing and able to identify at least one key area in which they can commit to making a change
- Open to finding a minimum of an hour of company time per week to speak with their coach (versus the "I just don't have time" attitude)
- Willing to share openly about themselves and their perceptions with someone outside the company
- Early adopters of new ideas/behaviors
- See themselves as trailblazers, risk takers, leaders
- Fundamentally proud of working at their organization

---

preparing that person for a more effective session. Guiding questions in this effort might include:

- What have I accomplished since our last session?
- What did I not get done that I wanted/thought I needed to?
- What challenges/problems am I facing now?
- What opportunities are available to me now?
- What do I most want to accomplish with my coach during our upcoming session?
- I want to use my coach to: _____
- I want to stay focused on: _____
- Actions I will take: _____

NOTE

All goals should be SMART: specific, measurable, actionable, reasonable (meaning it should be a challenge but not unachievable), and time-bound.

To help assure accomplishment of goals, the person being coached should consider the following:

- Milestones for each goal.
- Focus areas for change. For example, the person being coached might seek a change in behavior, habits, or lifestyle.
- Immediate action steps, if relevant.
- Agreement about how action plans and steps will be tracked and recorded.

A template for a coaching development plan is shown in Figure 3.1. Of course, each question can be customized for the person being coached, to achieve maximum clarity about exactly what will be accomplished and the net value of accomplishments. The clearer the person being coached is before launching into action, the easier it will be to assess the value of each accomplishment in pursuit of the goal. The plan provides a built-in feedback and learning loop.

If the person being coached is a linear, concrete thinker, he or she may want to fill out a plan personally. Others might not have the patience and will need the coach's direct assistance. Whichever method is used, the coach will need a clear, written plan to track activities and experiences along the way, and connect each new learning to the bigger picture.

Finally, the coach and person being coached must craft a coaching covenant, in which the coach agrees to be honest and courageous on behalf of the client's best interest and stated agenda, and the client agrees to give the coach direct feedback about the coaching experience to help him or her be the best possible coach. This is how a true partnership is created, and how the best work is facilitated.

THE SESSIONS

During the design and contracting stages the organization will often have specified the number of sessions that the coach and

Coaching Development Plan		
Vision for Coaching: (What does my [work, professional, personal] landscape look like as a result of coaching?)		
Development Needs:		
Areas to Leverage:		
Goals: Long Term (5–10 yrs), Short Term (2–3 yrs), Immediate (3 mos.–2 yrs.)		
SMART Goal #1		
Milestones		

Potential questions to make sure goal is SMART
What visible behaviors will change?
What action will you take to achieve the goal?
By what date will you achieve this goal?
Who will be impacted by the goal?
How will you know that the goal has been achieved?
What result do you expect in achieving this goal?
How will this impact the business?
What is the estimated impact in dollars to the business?

SMART Goal #2	
Milestones	

What visible behaviors will change?
What action will you take to achieve the goal?
By what date will you achieve this goal?
Who will be impacted by the goal?
How will you know the goal has been achieved?
What result do you expect in achieving this goal?
How will this impact the business?
What is the estimated impact in dollars to the business?

SMART Goal #3	
Milestones	

What visible behaviors will change?
What action will you take to achieve the goal?
By what date will you achieve this goal?
Who will be impacted by the goal?
What result do you expect in achieving this goal?
How will this impact the business?
What is the estimated impact in dollars to the business?

SMART Goal #4	
Milestones	

Figure 3.1

Coaching Development Plan

What visible behaviors will change?	
What action will you take to achieve the goal?	
By what date will you achieve this goal?	
Who will be impacted by the goal?	
How will you know the goal has been achieved?	
What result do you expect in achieving this goal?	
How will this impact the business?	
What is the estimated impact in dollars to the business?	
SMART Goal #5	
Milestones	
What visible behaviors will change?	
What action will you take to achieve the goal?	
By what date will you achieve this goal?	
Who will be impacted by the goal?	
How will you know the goal has been achieved?	
What result do you expect in achieving this goal?	
How will this impact the business?	
What is the estimated impact in dollars to the business?	

Figure 3.1

Coaching Development Plan (*Continued*)

person being coached are expected to have. For executive coaching, this will often be at least one or two coaching sessions per month for a minimum of 6 months. During each session, the person being coached should "check in with the big picture," for the purpose of connecting all conversations about day-to-day matters to the goals and focus areas. Accomplishments should be acknowledged and celebrated, and challenges used as opportunities to learn and grow. Unexpected problems or a sudden change in focus may necessitate reworking the goals. If this occurs, and it often does, the written documentation must reflect the changes. When goals are not reached during a coaching engagement, there should be a clear explanation.

Ideally, the coach will track the agenda for each session based on previous conversations, looping back to topics that both the coach and person being coached have agreed to revisit. The person being coached may also come to the session with an agenda, including such items as news to report, new information or requirements that may change the focus, or problems to solve. The coach's job is to work with the client to craft an agenda at the beginning of each call and manage the time so that every item is covered. Items that aren't covered can be deferred to the next session, and this should be tracked as well.

Each session should end with the person being coached having the opportunity to reflect on what was accomplished during the meeting and to identify to-do's before the next session. Coaches can follow up with reminder emails or calls between sessions.

Finally the coach and person being coached must agree on the time and place, if applicable, for the next session, to ensure there is no confusion. Such a strong sense of structure and continuity offers comfort to disciplined people and help for those less organized.

PREDICTABLE DISILLUSIONMENT

A rarely discussed but common occurrence for the person being coached generally occurs sometime between the fourth and seventh sessions with the coach. This assumes that at least 6 conversations are contracted, and often there are more. The individual usually begins the coaching engagement with a great deal of energy and enthusiasm, gains some early wins, and then loses steam as more difficult problems are tackled. This is predictable and normal. The coach needs to be ready for it so he or she can take the appropriate measures to ensure the person being coached isn't permanently demotivated when he or she "hits the wall."

Typically, disillusionment becomes apparent when the person being coached wants to change goals with no rational explanation, or says things such as, "This is harder than I thought," or "Maybe I should try something different."

When disillusionment occurs, the coach should first explain that it is normal, and that patience and persistence are required to get back on track. At this time, the coach should be ready to offer extra support, in the form of a pep talk for some and a challenge for others. The key is for the coach to be prepared and maintain faith in the client.

THE HONORABLE CLOSE

It can be difficult for both the coach and the person being coached to end a great coaching partnership. People facing the conclusion of their coaching relationships have been known to cancel sessions or miss them completely. This is often done in an effort to prolong the time that the person being coached can have the coach at his or her disposal.

The coach is responsible to guide the person being coached either to bring the partnership to an honorable close or to recontract for additional time. Recontracting for more time is common, and can be effective, but only if the goals needing the extra time are crystal clear to both parties. A client who is reluctant to give up the coach must be encouraged to examine what was gained from coaching and find alternative ways to provide that input and/or find appropriate mentors, managers, or colleagues to offer support going forward. Often, the coach can teach the person being coached how to walk through the coaching thought process him- or herself—that is, to be able to "go it alone."

Most coaches are delighted to be available for future coaching when the person is faced with a new challenge or transition that warrants additional support. It generally comforts the person being coached to know that the trusted coach will be available in the future, so that he or she will not have to go through the preliminaries all over again.

Finally, the person being coached must have a sense of what he or she gained from the coaching investment, and be clear about how to maximize the accomplishments moving forward. To do this, the coach should encourage the individual to answer these questions:

- What do I have now that I didn't have before?
- What habits have been changed, eliminated, or acquired?
- What do I want to continue to leverage?
- What do I need to be watchful of?
- How will I be sure I don't revert to doing things that no longer serve me well?
- How will I get support when I need it in the future?
- How will I know when to take a step back to gain perspective when I need it?

The successful coaching experience should not be a feel-good or abstract undertaking for the person being coached. It is the coach's job to manage the coaching experience and bring it to healthy closure. This allows the person being coached to understand the investment of time and energy, thereby vastly increasing the usefulness of the experience.

Taking Action

- How adept are you or your coaches at structuring the arc of the coaching relationship?
- Where might the coaching structure need to be strengthened?
- What will you do differently?

CHAPTER 4

Measuring the Success of Coaching in Your Company

EVEN THOUGH COACHING HAS BEEN taking place in organizations for several years, the research is just beginning to come in on the return on investment (ROI) for the process. Due to the time and the expense involved, to date, few studies have been done to measure the impact of coaching. However, several ways of measuring the success of coaching have emerged. This chapter looks at four approaches to measurement:

- Informal surveys
- Structured measurement interviews
- Formal impact studies
- Bottom-line dashboard tracking

IDENTIFYING CLEAR OBJECTIVES FOR THE COACHING INITIATIVE

As noted previously, before coaching is launched in an organization, it is critical to get senior-level buy-in and sponsorship, as well as to think about how success will be measured. Senior-level sponsorship strengthens the effectiveness of coaching, especially as the coaching is linked to leadership initiatives. Identifying clear linkages between coaching, senior leaders, organizational objectives, and leadership competencies helps to encourage commitment to and, thus, success from, the coaching process.

We've said this before, but it bears repeating: Before coaching success can be measured, clear objectives for it must be established. This is as true for coaching as it is for training or other organizational investments. Articulating clear objectives means defining success. Examples of clear objectives include:

- Increasing retention of key leaders by a minimum of 15 percent within the next 12 months.
- Improving morale by at least 5 percent, as evidenced by pre- and postinitiative surveys (postinitiative surveys might be three months after coaching has stopped).
- Increasing the number of one-on-one's with direct reports.
- Improving the quality of executive-level communication to managers, as reported by managers.

After they have been established, the objectives must be communicated to coaches and those being coached. Communication methods include: a series of email announcements (single emails are less effective than a series), a combination of email and voice messages, or a formal launch that brings all participants together. At the same time objectives are shared, they should be linked to senior-level leadership and organizational initiatives.

One of the most effective coaching launches in a Fortune 100 company brought all 40 participants together in one room along with the entire executive team. The CEO of the organization stood up first and said, "We are very pleased to be in the same room with you today to launch our first coaching initiative. Because you are the future of this organization, we want to invest in your career. We are offering coaching as a developmental resource, and we hope it serves you and our company well. We encourage each of you to speak with your managers and to identify three to five key areas to focus on with your coach. This is not intended to be punitive in any way. Rather, it's an investment in your development as a future leader of our company. One of our objectives for the coaching is to ensure that we have well-qualified, highly skilled leaders in the next few years. We hope you are one of those leaders."

In the preceding example, the launch was done during an on-site meeting, but the same information could have been communicated via voice message or email. The key is to have high-level leaders who communicate clearly their commitment to the coaching and the objectives it entails.

INFORMAL SURVEYS TO MEASURE SUCCESS

At the same time senior-level sponsorship and objectives are being identified, and as the coaching initiative is being launched, it's time to start thinking about measuring success. One way to gather data is to use online surveys, such as Survey Monkey (www.surveymonkey.com) and Zoomerang (www.info.zoomerang.com), as they are easy to send out to numerous people and to compile. Online surveys can be submitted anonymously or can include personal information.

Although surveys are most commonly sent out after coaching is completed, they can be prepared in advance so they are ready to send at predetermined times. Timing is everything. Consider when people are likely to complete the survey, and build in enough time to allow for at least one reminder, along with a link to the survey to those who haven't responded yet. Also consider how long after the completion of coaching you want to wait to gather information. Some organizations conduct their surveys within two weeks after the coaching initiative is completed. Others allow at least six to eight weeks between the end of the coaching initiative and when survey results are gathered. Be sure to identify as many dates as possible before the coaching is completed.

Sending surveys midway through the process is another way to gather data. If yours is a long-term coaching initiative—for example, executives are getting six months of coaching—this may be a useful approach to collect comprehensive data. Such a survey could ask specific questions related to the effectiveness of the coaching so far, the connection established between the person being coached and the coach, any new skills or development areas being addressed, early application in the workplace of knowledge learned from coaching so far, and so forth. Two questions frequently asked are: "Overall, how would you rate your coaching experience?" and "What are the top three things you are doing differently as a result of the coaching?"

**Sample Coaching Questions to Ask
Midway through the Process**

- How many coaching sessions have you completed?
- How effective do you consider your coaching to be to date?
- How satisfied are you with your coach?
- What is the primary focus of your coaching?
- How are you using your coaching within your role/job?
- What are the top three things you are doing differently as a result of your coaching?
- What would make your coaching experience more effective?
- Overall, how would you rate your coaching experience?

At the end of long-term coaching initiatives another survey can be distributed that includes some of the same questions along with others that are pertinent to the overall objectives. Subsequently, the data can be compiled and compared to check the progress (or lack of progress), as the coaching initiative proceeded.

It hardly needs to be said that the most effective surveys are those customized according to the needs of the organization and the desired information. Other survey preparation guidelines include:

- Keep them brief, with fewer than eight questions that take no more than 10 minutes to complete.

- Don't assume people will know how many questions or how much time it will take. Communicate the details.
- Tell participants that the time it will take to complete the survey is brief, so they are not daunted in advance.

NOTE

See the Sample Coaching Impact Report in Appendix II.

> **Making It Real**
>
> How might informal surveys be used in your organization to measure the success of training or other development activities?

STRUCTURED MEASUREMENT INTERVIEWS

Interviews are another good way to gather data, but they must be structured properly to ensure neither the questions nor the interviewer are slanted to preconceived outcomes. The interviews can be conducted within the organization or through an external party. One useful method of structured interviews is the Manchester approach,[1] which follows this process:

1. Talk with participants about the objectives for coaching, satisfaction with the coaching experience, and if they have achieved the objectives, new behaviors, and factors that contributed to the success (or failure) of the coaching process.
2. Ask participants to quantify one business impact. (Note: High-end estimates are limited to $1 million, so even if someone quantifies the impact at $6 million, it is converted to $1 million.)

3. Ask participants what percentage of the dollar impact they attribute to coaching, as compared to other factors (such as changes in the economic environment, industry changes, or other concurrent initiatives).
4. Ask participants to rate their confidence in that estimate. (Confidence levels usually range from 50 to 100 percent.)

Once this information has been gathered, subtract the cost of the coaching, and divide the total by the cost of the coaching initiative. Once that number has been determined, multiply the amount by 100 percent to obtain an ROI percentage, representing an adjusted ROI. (In fact, the ROI has been adjusted several times in order to maximize the credibility of the data.) See Figure 4.1.

As Gary, a key employee in a retail company, was becoming disgruntled, he was invited to receive six months of coaching. At the end of the period, Gary was invited to participate in an interview process to assess ROI of the coaching process. During the interview, Gary shared one of his key outcomes: "There was a change between my boss and me. I went from being frustrated, unhappy, and ready to leave, to capable and confident. My boss doesn't handle employee challenges for me anymore. My coach helped me to see how to do things differently. Coaching helped a lot. I needed the coach to 'get in my face'; and at times I needed more support. I got both from my coach. I got what I needed when I needed it."

When asked to put a label on the change he had experienced, Gary described it as "the retention of a key employee," and quantified it at $120,000, which covered rehiring and training a new person. Gary was then asked to share what percentage he attributed to coaching;

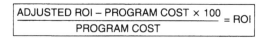

$$\frac{\text{ADJUSTED ROI} - \text{PROGRAM COST} \times 100}{\text{PROGRAM COST}} = \text{ROI}$$

Figure 4.1
The Manchester Formula[1]

he replied, "Sixty percent." When asked to rate his confidence in that percentage, Gary said it was easily 80 percent. In taking these numbers through the Manchester formula, and subtracting the cost of the coaching, the ROI was over 397 percent.

The Manchester approach can include an additional step. It would be easy to check in with Gary's manager to find out his perspective on what changes took place in Gary as a result of his being coached. Note, however, that interviews with other people to corroborate information take a few minutes and need to be carefully structured so as not to bias the interviewee.

Making It Real

How could structured measurement interviews be used in your organization to measure the success of training or other development activities?

THE FORMAL IMPACT STUDY

Impact studies are significantly more formal than surveys or structured measurement interviews. Based on the Success Case Methodology[2] pioneered by Robert Brinkerhoff, impact studies have a formalized process, which includes examining data based on the objectives of the coaching initiative (with or without a formal training program), the people who embraced coaching and moved forward significantly, and the people for whom coaching was not as effective. One assumption when developing such studies is that the impact of coaching is variable, and is dependent on how much was learned and how the knowledge was applied on the job. This gives important information leading to critical factors in the organization, which encourages (or discourages) application of the new knowledge.

IMPACT STUDY PROCESS

Whenever a formal impact study is undertaken, the first step is to understand the coaching process. This includes the objectives and timing for the coaching initiative. Knowing why coaching was launched can be helpful in understanding critical factors in the organization at the time of coaching. In addition, knowing how many coaching sessions each person receives, in conjunction with each person's area of responsibility, is important.

After the aforementioned information is gathered, a survey is sent to all participants to gather pertinent data about the coaching initiative. More importantly, based on the survey responses, approximately 10 percent of participants are selected for a formal telephone interview of approximately 20 minutes about their coaching experience. The interviews and subsequent collation of the interview data can be done internally or externally. For the most objective results, it is best to use an outside person who is trained in the methodology and who can present a final report.

During the telephone interviews, participants are asked to identify specific ways coaching has affected their personal effectiveness and their business results. For many, coaching has a significant impact. However, it is common for some people to feel they have not benefited from the coaching experience, and this data is equally important. Either way, all participants are asked to think through the factors that contributed to the success or lack of success of the coaching process. Data from the interviews reveal not only what happened but also how it happened. Based on all the data, critical factors shown to have either facilitated or impeded success can be culled. These key factors are important to know, as they can be applied subsequently to other initiatives (training and/or coaching) within the organization.

From the data in the interviews, the leadership or business impact is determined, along with the bottom-line value of the coaching initiative. In addition, formal impact studies include sections on key findings and recommendations that help inform the organization on how to better leverage its investment in participants going through other workplace learning activities, including training and coaching.

NOTE

See Appendix II for a sample formal impact report.

Making It Real

How could a formal impact study be used in your organization to measure the success of training or other development activities?

TRACKING THE DASHBOARD

Some organizations measure ROI simply by tracking the change in bottom-line business results, otherwise known as the *dashboard*. Every business tracks a set of numbers to consistently assess the health of the company. These numbers can include employee satisfaction survey results, retention, sales increases, employee absenteeism, shrinkage, promotions, raises, bonuses, and more. Perhaps they are called *key productivity indicators, health indicators*, or the *monthly index*. Regardless, the success of coaching, to the extent that the coaching is designed to alter any significant number, can be assessed by a change (hopefully, for the better) on the dashboard. This is straightforward and easy to do (if measurement systems are already in place), and provides data that can be tracked over years. Like any of the ROI data discussed here, the dashboard analysis can be second-guessed, and is useful when bottom-line numbers are critical for measuring success.

> One organization discovered from its annual employee satisfaction survey scores that two areas—satisfaction with developmental opportunities and manager relationship—yielded consistently poor results. The organization was already providing all managers with basic management training, which focused on building the competency "developing others," as defined by the company. As a result of the low satisfaction scores, the organization's leadership decided to provide six months of coaching to all managers who had completed the training. Following this initiative, employee satisfaction experienced a small but historically significant increase the following year. The organization's senior leadership felt that the ROI had been proven sufficiently.

Another organization that commissioned a full impact study also tracked bottom-line business results as part of its ROI measure. Doing this can be fairly simple, especially in sales organizations where sales numbers are tracked consistently. Other numbers can be tracked, too, if enough people receive coaching. Numbers such as retention, promotions, and performance review scores can be examined for increases. In one organization, the coaching initiative was designed specifically to help regional managers improve their hiring skills and increase hiring. The results were easy to track.

The major challenge with using dashboard numbers to prove ROI is that coaching is only one of several variables. One client, whose churn (loss of qualified sales managers) was reduced by a staggering 67 percent during a time when all organizational senior leaders received coaching, agreed that the coaching had been a good experience, but pointed to another variable that he thought played a larger role in the reduction in churn. The client said: "This coaching has been without exception the best development initiative I have seen in my 20-year career, but let's face it, the dot-com bubble burst and the economy hit the skids in the meantime, so I can't give all the credit for churn reduction to coaching." Dashboard numbers are clearly impacted by so many internal and external forces that they can be tricky as an ROI indicator unless they are held up against the dashboard of a comparable control group that is subject to the same variables but receives no coaching.

Making It Real

How could tracking the dashboard be done in your organization to measure the success of training or other development activities?

FINAL THOUGHTS

Regardless of how ROI is determined, more and more organizations are interested in measuring the impact and success of training and developmental activities, including coaching. Each of the four approaches described in this chapter has pros and cons. For example, while surveys are inexpensive and can be used to gather anecdotal information rather quickly, they are usually brief and limited in scope. And whereas structured measurement interviews can be done internally, and are low cost, they are time-consuming for both the interviewer and participants. Finally, formal impact studies are thorough and methodical in gathering information and relating it to the organization, but they are usually conducted by third parties and, therefore, are much more expensive. In organizations where collection and tracking of dashboard numbers are already being done, this method proves to be a simple way to determine the ROI of coaching, though its validity can be easily disputed.

Each of these methods can be used separately or in combination to gather data. For example, some companies use surveys and interviews together. Others use a dashboard approach to find out what exactly happened during the coaching initiative, with the key factors identified at the onset of coaching, along with surveys to find out how the coaching worked. Still other companies focus on only one method for determining ROI.

To assess which way to go in your company, think about the objectives you will use for measuring the coaching initiative, the value of the data, and how the data will be used. If the data needs to be formalized for a board presentation or to determine a larger role for coaching services at leadership levels, then a formal impact study may be warranted. One organization that measured the impact of coaching on leadership retention and development used a series of formal impact studies to prove that retention had increased substantially, thereby providing a foundation for the organization to continue with leadership coaching.

If the data is needed to prove that internal coaching is effective after training, then a survey may be adequate. In several organizations, there was concern that coaching might not really make a difference as a follow-up to training. In each case, a pilot was conducted to measure the effectiveness of coaching. The pilot was set up so that half of the participants received coaching and half did not. In several organizations, the participants who received coaching were self-selected, and in others they were selected either by HR or their managers. In one company, classroom participants voted on who was most "coachlike," and those people received the coaching. In all pilots, the survey results showed that coaching made a noticeable difference in how the knowledge was applied on the job.

If requests have been made for hard ROI numbers, the structured measurement interviews may be the best approach. These interviews are focused specifically on where coaching made a difference, as well as the bottom-line monetary value of that difference. In one organization, conducting the structured interviews proved that the objectives for coaching had been met many times over. In fact, in this organization, approximately 75 percent of participants requested additional coaching sessions after they had already received five months of coaching.

ROI data is useful and important, especially during periods of economic downturns and reduced variable expenses. The key is to identify what can be measured and then measure it! Equally important is finding respected senior leaders who, as a result of being coached, have experienced tremendous personal and professional growth, as observed by others, and who become coaching champions for the benefits of coaching to the organization.

Taking Action

- Where is your organization currently in terms of measuring the success of training or other development programs?
- Where does your organization need to be in terms of measuring the success of training or other development programs?
- What steps can you take to move your organization forward?

NOTES

1. Joy McGovern, "Maximizing the Impact of Executive Coaching: Behavioral Change, Organizational Outcomes, and Return on Investment," *The Manchester Review* (Vol. 6, 2001): 1–9.
2. Robert Brinkerhoff, *The Success Case Method: Find Out Quickly What's Working and What's Not* (San Francisco: Barrett-Koehler, 2003).

PART II

Coaching Skills and Techniques

CHAPTER 5

The Coaching Process and Basic Coaching Skills

A CARPENTER LOOKS AT a bare wall and builds functional and beautiful cabinetry. An artist looks at a blank canvas and creates an expressive masterpiece. A teacher looks at an impressionable child and instills a lifelong love for learning.

The carpenter, artist, and teacher, in practicing their diverse disciplines, have mastered the skills and honed the processes necessary to ensure they are effective at what they do. Similarly, an effective coach, whether internal or external, uses a variety of skills and a proven process when working with organizations. Depending on what will be most beneficial for the person being coached, an effective coach uses one skill or another, and often uses several simultaneously. He or she also adjusts the coaching process to best match the needs of the person being coached.

As stated earlier, coaching is a deliberate process that helps others to move forward toward achieving their goals. This chapter presents a coaching process and explores four core coaching skills that can easily be adapted to each person's needs and situation. The information in this chapter can be used by coaches and by managers and leaders who are using coaching skills.

THE C-FAR COACHING PROCESS

Coaching is a defined and deliberate process. As anyone in the corporate world knows, a defined process can make the

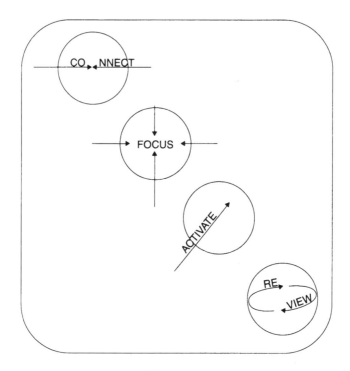

Figure 5.1
The C-FAR Process

difference between randomly presented and time-wasting meetings and efficient and productive meetings. Although many process models exist, we have found the C-FAR coaching process, which stands for connect, focus, activate, review (shown in Figure 5.1) to be both simple and effective.[1]

In addition to being an excellent method to use for coaching, the C-FAR process is also useful for leading and managing individuals and teams. It helps keep individuals and teams involved, focused, action-oriented, and clear about next steps.

In the following subsections, we'll go through the four stages of C-FAR in turn.

CONNECT

Does it seem that no one has time for small talk anymore at work? This is not surprising, given ongoing changes and reductions in personnel in many companies today. One result is that few people have time to truly connect with one another anymore. In a *Fortune* magazine article titled, "Why CEOs Fail," research showed that one reason CEOs fail is because they don't demonstrate that they care about their employees. One way to communicate caring is to make an effort to connect with others, even briefly. As noted in the article, "The motto of the successful CEO, worthy of inscription on his or her office wall, is, 'People first, strategy second.'"[2] The connect component of the C-FAR process is simple, yet requires discipline. Making an effort to connect with those being coached models how to build rapport and set the context. This is often overlooked both in coaching and in leading.

Connecting can include asking simple questions or making statements to demonstrate attentiveness and interest. For example:

- How was your birthday weekend?
- I understand that the sales team was excited about the presentation you prepared for them. Congratulations!
- It has been a long time since our last meeting, and you've taken on three big new clients. What has been most interesting about them?
- I've heard really good things about your work these days, and that you're doing well facing some major challenges.

Each of these statements or questions is focused on the person being coached or managed and communicates interest in him or her. Each shows in simple ways that the coach/manager cares.

In one company, Tim, a high-potential manager, told his manager, Nick, that he didn't know why his team didn't think he cared about them. He admitted that he wasn't interested in what they did during the weekends or holidays, and said he was only interested in whether they showed up for work and did their jobs. Pressed further by Nick, Tim acknowledged that he started his Monday team meetings by immediately asking for agenda items, that he did not take time for small talk, to connect on a personal level.

Over the course of several conversations with Nick, Tim also admitted that he didn't know anything about most of the people on his team, but agreed to pay more attention to them from now on. For Tim, this meant that he would say hello in the mornings and ask about weekend or holiday activities. Two weeks later, when Tim came to a meeting with Nick, he said that he couldn't believe the difference in his staff—they seemed more open to him than ever before. Tim recognized that his simple greetings and questions communicated that he cared.

A key quality of the connect segment of the coaching process is openness. Being open means that the manager or the coach is interested in getting to know the other person, wants to hear what the person says, is willing to share him- or herself, and is truly present during the conversation. Being present and focused communicates openness and interest in the other person. One way to confirm there is a good connection is to answer the question, "Does the person I'm coaching know that I'm interested and that I care?"

FOCUS

How many times have you left a conversation knowing that you haven't talked about what's most important? Coaching helps the person being coached focus specifically on the most important topics and goals.

Effective coaching requires that the manager or the coach is attentive, probing to establish the most important focus for the person being coached. Getting to a clear and precise focal point can take up to half of a coaching conversation, yet it yields the best return on the time investment.

Good focusing questions include the following:

- What is the most pressing issue for you right now?
- What specifically do you need to get clear about?
- We have about 15 minutes to talk right now. What do you need?
- How can this conversation be most useful to you right now?

Consider this sample focusing dialogue between a manager and his/her report.

Manager: What's on your mind today, Marci?

Marci: I have so much going on. I need to focus on the Web site deadline—that's a challenge—and I want to talk about what's going on with Lucy, the team member who has been so difficult lately. And I think you've heard that the marketing meeting last week didn't go well. I need to follow up with two of the people who were there.

Manager: [thinking that it would be easy to suggest a direction, yet wanting to let Marci see it on her own] Which is most pressing right now?

Marci: I need to think through how to approach the two people from the marketing meeting. James wouldn't allow anyone else to speak, and he was being much more directive than usual. Loren didn't help at all. He was being argumentative, and so we couldn't get any traction.

Manager: [still trying to identify the focus] You've just mentioned several areas we could focus on: the meeting in general; James; Loren; and the fact that you weren't able to get any traction. Which direction shall we go in this conversation?

Marci: Let's talk about what's going on with James. He was not his usual self, and I'm concerned that he doesn't recognize his impact on the team. I really need to talk with him today.

Manager: [wanting to confirm the immediate focus] Sounds like a good plan to take the next few minutes to talk about James and his impact on the team. What are you considering as you approach him?

To use coaching skills effectively and efficiently, it's important to be alert and agile enough to change direction, as needed. One question to ask that helps to determine whether this step of the coaching process has been met is, "Did we confirm the specific focus?" (See Figure 5.2.)

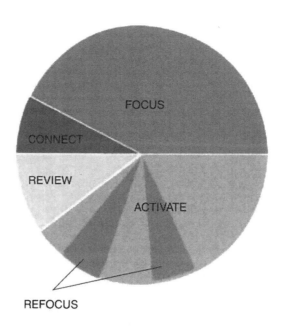

Figure 5.2
Establishing, Confirming, and Reestablishing Focus

ACTIVATE

Coaching without intentional action is just another conversation! Taking intentional action includes determining specific actions that are well suited to the project or goal being discussed. Taking action includes taking the time to think, observe others, and determine strategy and tactics.

Effective coaching helps people determine, then take, intentional, meaningful actions. Once the actions are determined, the manager or coach asks questions to help anchor the action and ensure accountability, removal of obstacles, and positive outcomes. Activating questions might include, "What will you do when you encounter that obstacle?" "How will you keep moving forward even if the other person doesn't cooperate?" "What else do you need in order to take that action?"

When coaching, it is important to be courageous in challenging the person being coached to think through the intended actions. For example, "Kat, what possible ramifications might there be to that course of action?" Or, "Kat, if those interviews don't go as well as expected, what is your plan B?" This stage can involve worst-case scenario thinking or examining faulty assumptions. Worst-case scenario thinking is a useful tool that simply involves asking the question: "What is the worst thing that can happen, and how can you be prepared for that?"

Sometimes coaching requires having to provoke the person to expand their personal expectations by asking him or her to think bigger or more strategically. For example, "Kat, how do these short-term decisions fit our two-year plan?" Or, "Kat, being a great manager is a wonderful goal. What about becoming a great leader?"

Similarly, coaching may require the manager or coach to redirect the conversation to encourage the person to fully reach his or her personal potential. "Kat, your own goals sound very aggressive. How do they fit with the team goals?" Or, "Something is different. What is going on that is causing you to make a decision against your best instincts?"

Several questions that encourage action are as follows:

- What options are you considering?
- What will you do first? Next?
- Who needs to be included in this decision so you can move forward smoothly?
- How will you know that you are on track? What evidence will let you know you are being successful?
- What might throw you off track? How will you know you are being derailed?

In this conversation, Marci and her manager continue to talk, to solidify Marci's actions going forward.

Manager: What approach are you considering when you talk with James?

Marci: I really want James to consider his impact on the team, but I'm not sure how to get started. I know that I was frustrated because we really needed to forge ahead last week. I want to tone it down a bit so that the conversation is a good one.

Manager: [wanting to go into some communication dynamics, but knowing it's too soon] What would a "good" conversation sound like?

Marci: I'd be able to talk without any anger or frustration coming through. I'd ask questions that show interest, so that James would know I really want to understand what he's doing.

Manager: That sounds great. How can you get ready for this conversation?

Marci: Maybe I need to write down my concerns and some possible outcomes. And I need to think about what questions to ask. I'll make a list of questions that I can keep in the back of my mind.

Manager: What else?

Marci:	I really want to understand what's going on with James so I can work more effectively with him. I want to hear what's going on. Wow, this seems much more genuine now.
Manager:	Yes, it really does seem like something has shifted in you. What's next?

The "activate" segment includes speaking courageously—that is, saying what needs to be said. Speaking simply and directly, the manager or coach becomes a tremendous thought partner, totally focused on the other's success. To confirm that this part of the coaching process has been completed, answer the question: "What actions need to be taken?"

REVIEW

We've all had the experience of concluding a conversation thinking we have reached a mutual understanding only to find out later (sometimes, too late) that we were mistaken. We've all been in meetings at which there was no review at the conclusion to reiterate decisions made. This has led to having subsequent meetings that covered essentially the same ground, because no one did what was expected of them. Unfortunately, reviewing rarely happens either in team or individual meetings. It takes very little time to review, yet doing so can make the difference between successful and unsuccessful meetings.

In the coaching process, as in meetings, it is critical to include a few minutes for review in order to reach agreement on next steps and to ensure success and forward motion.

Several effective review questions include the following:

- What will you do between now and our next conversation?
- What actions will you take? By when?
- What do you still need? (Not, "What do you need *from me?*" as that redirects the focus and responsibility.)
- What was most useful to you in this conversation?

When the executive director of a large nonprofit organization heard about the review part of the coaching process, he immediately committed to including a time for review in every meeting he scheduled. Three weeks later, he shared the following with his team, "Before our classes on coaching, I was so frustrated that our meetings seemed to cover the same ground over and over. Then I heard about the review stage of coaching. I committed to myself to include this important component in every meeting. Many of you may have noticed that at the end of *all* my meetings I ask the team or the individual to go over their commitments, rather than telling them what to do. As a result, commitment levels have increased, and my meetings have changed. People are doing what they say they'll do in the time frame that's been determined. I feel like we're finally moving ahead!"

In a coaching or meeting setting, those responsible for the actions discussed, rather than the coach or leader, should do the review. Think about the difference between being told what to do, and by when, and stating yourself what you'll do. It is a very different experience. The probability for follow-through increases when people themselves state their actions and timelines, rather than being told what these are.

Effective coaching models asking the other person to do the review. One question that can help determine whether a review is needed or has been completed is, "Are there clear agreements, which include timelines?" If not, ask the person being coached to go over his or her intended actions, and don't hesitate to ask "by when" as needed.

Making It Real

Think about the stages of a coaching conversation: connect, focus, activate, and review.

- In which areas are you strong, and which need more attention?
- What will you do to include each stage of the coaching process in future conversations?

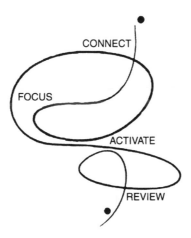

Figure 5.3
The Iterative Nature of the C-FAR Process

C-FAR as an Iterative Process

Although the C-FAR coaching process includes distinct stages, it is iterative rather than linear (see Figure 5.3). For although there may be an initial time to connect and focus, for example, it is common to circle back to connect at some point. Even more common is to move back and forth between focusing and activating.

Taking time to focus and refocus is vital in the coaching process. Often, after an initial focus has been determined, the coach or manager realizes quickly that it isn't the true focus area. Thus, it is important to linger in or revisit the focus segment, as needed.

CORE COACHING SKILLS

The C-FAR coaching process is the "what" of coaching. Core coaching skills are the "how" of the conversation. The coaching process may be analogized to the bones of the conversation, and the coaching skills to the ligaments that hold the bones together.

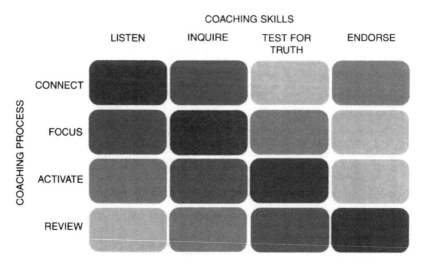

Figure 5.4
Core Coaching Skills and Process

Without the ligaments, the bones fall apart. Likewise, without coaching skills, the process falls apart. How the coaching skills and process connect depends on what is occurring during the conversation.

Like the coaching process, coaching skills are simple, yet difficult. Often, in coaching classes, students will say, "This is not nearly as easy as it appears!" So, what are the core coaching skills? The easiest way to remember them is by the acronym LITE, for: listen, inquire, test for truth, endorse. As depicted in Figure 5.4, certain skills are more heavily concentrated (depicted with darker shading) during certain parts of the coaching conversation, as follows:

- When *connecting*, the primary skills are listening and inquiring.
- When *focusing*, the primary skills are inquiring and listening.
- When getting people to take *action*, the skills include testing for truth and inquiring.
- In the *review* component of the coaching process, the primary skills are endorsing and testing for truth.

The subsections that follow explore each of these skills in greater depth.

LISTEN

Most people think they are listening well when they are not interrupting and are making eye contact. The truth is, it's much more than that, and listening is something most people do poorly, indeed.

Think of the many distractions that pull your mind away from another person when he or she is speaking to you, whether on the phone or in person. Perhaps it's the emails you know that are piling up, or the phone calls that need to be returned. Maybe it's the groceries you have to remember to pick up on the way home from work, or your child from school, by 4:00. Are you worrying about that deadline looming ever closer, or the sales target you're missing by a mile this quarter?

Everyone is distracted as they are required to multitask their way through their workdays. Unfortunately, getting lost in that shuffle is the critical skill of listening. For coaching to be effective, a manager or coach must learn to be fully present and focused when listening to the person being coached. Knowing how to quiet the mind is necessary in order to truly hear all that is being said.

What Keeps You from Listening Attentively?

- Thinking you know what the other person is going to say?
- Pressure of your to-do list?
- Boredom?
- Lack of interest or caring?
- Email ping, phone ringing, noise in the hallway, electronics flashing?
- Thinking about personal chores?
- Worrying about the mortgage?
- Wondering when you can take the car in to get fixed?
- Health concerns?

- Daydreaming?
- Planning for the next conversation or meeting?
- What else?

For more than a month, Barrie and her manager talked about her need to listen, to really listen, to her team members when they were talking to her. Barrie described how frustrating it was to try and keep herself from multitasking, especially when she thought about how much she had to do. On this particular call with her manager, Barrie said, "I don't have time to listen. I have more important things to do." Her manager encouraged her to take a few minutes each day to be present and focused in at least one conversation.

When Barrie connected with her manager a few weeks later, she announced, "You're not going to believe what happened! After our last meeting, I was walking to another office and met up with a colleague I haven't seen in seven years. I greeted him and asked how he was doing. He said, 'This has been the worst day in all my 14 years at this company.' "

Barrie continued, "I could hear your words in my mind, 'Just listen a few seconds longer. Listen to understand what he's really saying.' He talked for five minutes, which seemed endless. But I didn't interrupt once. The last thing he said to me was, 'Thank you so much for listening. I really needed to talk about this, and I'm not sure what I would have done if you hadn't asked and listened.' I saw such a difference in him in just five minutes! I think I get it!"

Making It Real

Want to improve your listening skills? Try this: The next time someone is talking to you and your mind begins to wander, be intentional about repeating in your mind each word the other person is saying, at the same time the person is saying them. See if you can track, word for word, along with the person who's speaking. Practice this often to improve both your listening and coaching skills.

To fully listen, you, the listener, are required to be fully present and focused on what the other person is saying. At the same time, listen to learn about the other person and from the other person. This means listening with an open mind, suspending judgments. Listen as if you were willing to be influenced. You don't have to be influenced, but you will definitely listen differently if you are willing to learn and be influenced.

Listening prompts:

- How have things been going?
- Say more about that.
- What else are you thinking?
- How did _____ go?
- That sounds really intriguing. . . .

INQUIRE

Inquiring is asking questions that promote discovery for the other person. Effective coaching means listening well in order to be able to ask precise and focused questions. In short, inquiring and listening go hand in hand when coaching (see Figure 5.5).

Typically, most people ask questions when they are interested in the subject or when they are curious about something. When

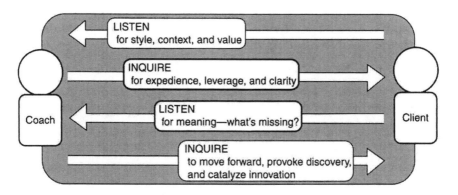

Figure 5.5
Inquiring and Listening

Table 5.1

Effective and Ineffective Coaching Questions

Avoid These Questions That Focus on the Coach	Ask These Questions That Focus on the Person Being Coached
What have you already done? The person being coached knows what he or she has already done, so the question is more for the coach than the person being coached.	What have you done that can inform your next steps? This question draws on the past to move forward.
Why did you think that? The person being coached already knows the "why," so the answer to this is more for the coach than the person being coached.	What are you thinking now as you move forward? This question helps the person gain clarity and focuses him or her on what's next.
How did that make you feel? This question focuses on the past rather than on moving forward.	What do you need to know to make the decision? This question focuses on collecting what is needed to make a sound decision.

it comes to coaching, however, inquiring is done for the express purpose of moving the other person toward effective, intentional action. Coaches should take care to avoid asking questions for their own benefit. Questions posed in the context of a coaching session should always be for the benefit of the person being coached. Table 5.1 lists questions of both types, as a guide for coaches.

When inquiring, focus on the "what," "how," and "when," to move forward. These words create an environment for the person being coached to think about what can be done. Just be careful

Table 5.2

Leading versus Discovery Coaching Questions

Avoid Leading Questions	Ask Questions That Promote Discovery
What if you call these three people and ask for their data? This is advice, wrapped in a "what" question.	What are you thinking of doing next? Who might to be able to help?
How about if you talk to Sam first thing tomorrow morning? This is leading, wrapped in a "how" question.	When will you talk with Sam?
Would it be helpful to ask Lara to take over the team meeting for you so you can be at the board meeting? This is offering a solution, wrapped in a "would it be helpful" question.	If that board meeting is so important, what can you do to make sure you can be there?

not to use these words to lead the person into the direction you think is best. Inquiry should always promote discovery on the part of the person being coached, so that he or she maintains responsibility for the outcomes. Table 5.2 lists leading versus discovery questions.

TEST FOR TRUTH

Testing for truth is the skill a coach uses to accelerate forward motion in those being coached. Think about when someone said something to you that shifted your perspective or your behaviors. Maybe a trusted coworker said, "The choice is really yours," and that simple statement caused you to realize that you had choices. Maybe your boss said, "No more apologizing," and you woke up to the fact that you didn't have to apologize anymore. Perhaps a senior executive said, "It's time to lead, not manage" and you were challenged to step into leadership in a new way. Chances are that you remember exactly where you were and even what you were wearing when you heard these test-for-truth messages—which most likely contained seven words or fewer!

The test-for-truth skill, when used effectively, facilitates a seismic shift in the perception of the person being coached. It is accomplished through the delivery of concise, small packages of information, seven words or fewer, sometimes presented as an observation and sometimes said with a bit of an edge—but not sarcasm or criticism, neither of which is ever appropriate. The intent should always be to prompt the person to think in a different way, to take a new perspective, to practice new behaviors, or all three. A test-for-truth message properly timed, well positioned, and submitted with compassion, whether said with an edge or delivered as a gentle observation, can have a galvanic impact.

When Taz was a small boy, he stole things. Mostly, he stole little items like gum or candy, but as he got older he acquired a reputation for not being trusted because of his stealing. One day when Taz was 15, two of his buddies came up to him and said, "Taz, we don't want to be your friends anymore. You steal things. Stop stealing." They walked away, and Taz was shocked.

During the course of the next month, Taz found out that his father was being transferred to another city, which meant a move for his family. Word spread at Taz's school about the upcoming move. His two buddies approached Taz again. "Taz, you're moving. You have a fresh start. Never steal again." [Notice the three sentences, all fewer than five words, which Taz never forgot.]

Taz shared his story with colleagues and direct reports at a meeting in his company when he was learning about the test-for-truth skill.

He ended his story by saying that he would never be where he was today if it hadn't been for his buddies speaking truth to him.

Today, Taz is a senior leader in his company. Recently, a team member arrived in his office presenting a complex challenge that she was struggling with. As she spoke, Taz recognized she was speaking in all-or-nothing terms. So, he casually said, "No more all-or-nothing thinking, Becky. Think in terms of both/and." As a result of those short, pithy statements, Becky saw a different way of approaching the situation that was worth trying. She thanked Taz and walked out of his office.

Testing for truth is a powerful skill that is intended to thrust people to a new level of awareness or behavior. Think about airplanes as they are taking off. They reach a point at which the thrust pushes them up off the runway, causing them to be airborne. The thrust is just enough to get them into the air but not too much, to prevent the plane going straight up or looping over backward. It moves the plane forward on a trajectory that takes it higher and higher. Testing-for-truth messages are just like the jet taking off with just the right amount of thrust.

When delivering test-for-truth messages, think in terms of seven words or fewer, delivered in a neutral way that doesn't inflict damage on the other person. This number of words makes the best impact because people can remember easily what they have just been told.

The statements or questions are neutral in that they aren't pushed at or forced upon the person. If the person being coached doesn't "bite" on the message, it can be retracted or left hanging.

In telling her HR professional, Tami, about a challenging situation with a colleague, Carolyn described all of the actions she was taking. When Tami asked what the colleague was doing, Carolyn replied, "Not much." Wanting to get her attention and shift her awareness to just how much more Carolyn was doing than her colleague, Tami responded slowly, "*You* have to do *all* the work?" Carolyn responded, "Yes, and I feel great that I've done so much to try to get this sorted out." Carolyn took the comment as an endorsement, rather than a test-for-truth message, which was the intent. Tami, while surprised, let it pass without further comment at that time. Later, however, she looped back to it.

Sometimes, the message is delivered in a way that hurts the other person, and unintentional damage is done. When that happens, it is important to notice the negative impact, apologize as soon as possible, and take responsibility for the mistake.

During one traumatic coaching conversation, Connie seemed to be thinking only of herself, as she described her workload and her discouragement with her team. After several minutes of listening and asking questions to promote discovery about this circumstance, Darlene, Connie's coach, said, "You're choosing to stay in the department. You can go elsewhere in the company. Remember, you have choices!" Connie was shocked and very upset by these comments. In no uncertain terms, Connie told Darlene that Darlene had expressed zero compassion or understanding of the situation and that she didn't want to continue their coaching sessions.

Darlene, surprised by the force of Connie's response, sent Connie an email saying that it was not her intent to hurt her. Rather, Darlene wrote, she had hoped that her comments would inspire Connie to think through the choices she had. That was her only aim; not to hurt Connie. Darlene let Connie know how sorry she was for the impact her comments had and apologized for damaging the relationship. Several weeks later, Connie contacted Darlene and asked when they could reconnect. The words, "You have choices," had penetrated.

Sometimes, it is the content of the conversation that causes the damage; other times, it is the tone or delivery. In the preceding example, Darlene tried to clarify her intent and apologized for the unintentional impact it had. Whenever there is a misalignment of intent and impact, an apology is one of the best ways (maybe, the only way) to enable the relationship to continue. And be aware that it may take a few days or even weeks for the person being coached to realize that truth was spoken, and to accept the statements as they were intended. In this case, it took several weeks for Connie to see the truth in what Darlene had said, especially that she had choices.

Making It Real

- How do you handle miscommunications?
- How quickly do you "clean up the mess" when something goes awry?
- What can you do to become aware quickly of hurtful situations and begin the recovery process more expeditiously?

Test-for-truth messages can be the most efficient way to accelerate people into new levels of awareness and action, but they *can* cause damage. Nevertheless, it is worth the risk to speak up, especially when there are options (apologizing and taking responsibility) for reestablishing the relationship, should that be necessary.

ENDORSE

The fourth coaching skill to develop is endorsing others. To endorse is distinct from offering positive feedback or praising, both of which have their place. The dictionary indicates that to endorse means to:

1. Pay attention, and officially mark that attention has been paid.
2. Validate the existence of.
3. Approve that something or someone is what they appear to be.
4. Publicly state support and sanction.

To understand endorsing, think back to the last time someone told you what he or she appreciated about you, or when someone noticed something positive you did and shared his or her acknowledgment. How did you respond after receiving the endorsement? If the compliment was genuine, probably you felt energized.

Too often, however, people think they are endorsing, but they are really talking about themselves. For example, when two colleagues are talking together, one might say, "I really appreciated that I could talk with you yesterday." This is clearly focused on the speaker, not the person being endorsed. Instead, notice how the following statement focuses on the person being endorsed: "Thank you so much for the time yesterday. Your feedback and input were hugely helpful."

Making It Real

Try to remove the word "I" from your endorsements. Start instead with "you," and limit self-references.

Endorsing is a simple skill, focused on energizing the other person. Endorsements can be shared privately in an email; through a voice message; in a handwritten note; or publicly, by copying others, in team meetings, in companywide publications either online or in print. Before you send an endorsement, however, be sure to take into consideration how the other person prefers to be endorsed. To determine this, take note whether the individual is more introverted or extroverted, if he or she seems to like public displays of attention or is more private in nature. Watch to see if the person communicates individually with others or tends to be vocal at team meetings. That is, pay attention to subtle indicators of personal preferences. The key point is that to endorse properly requires that you pay close attention, and the net result is that the person being coached feels seen and heard.

In addition, when determining how to share an endorsement, keep in mind three critical components of endorsing: an endorsement must be genuine, timely, and specific.

Genuine

Everyone can tell when someone says something that isn't genuine. It comes across as self-serving, either by the words or by the tone. When a person is genuine, there is no doubt that the purpose of what he or she is saying is all about the person to whom it is directed. The purpose of a genuine endorsement is to give credit where credit is due. Teams that acknowledge when someone does something well are stronger because their members know that they are appreciated.

Timely

When someone does something well, endorse the person as soon as possible; do not wait. The impact of timely appreciation is energizing; otherwise, often it's forgotten when it's not shared immediately. Try to endorse within 24 hours of noticing a job well done.

Keep in mind that it is equally important to notice when small advances are made, as well as when major projects are completed on time or under budget. Ken Blanchard and his coauthors draw attention to this point in their book *Whale Done: The Power of Positive Relationships*.[3] When whales at Sea World are learning to do tricks, they are given immediate feedback each time they accomplish a small step toward the goal, say, jumping or spinning. When they jump a little higher or spin at exactly the right time, the trainer throws a fish into their mouths. In this way, they receive the message immediately that they have done what was wanted. If the trainer delayed the feedback, chances are the whales would not connect the reward, the fish, with the action they took.

Specific

Have you ever completed a project only to have someone say, "Nice job." Period. Nothing more. What if, instead, you were told: "Wow, you completed that project on time, and included so many pertinent details and a comprehensive timeline. Very nice job." It makes a difference to hear exactly what is appreciated. In fact, it is energizing to know how to replicate a job well done, and some of those details can come through the endorsement.

Joe is known as a man who loves his job and is a model for performance at a high level. He volunteers whenever a project is suited to his skills, and he encourages others whenever he can. But Joe hasn't always been that way. Years ago, he was a ho-hum performer who embodied apathy and had considered leaving his company. At the time, he worked for a man who was known as a results-driven, hard-hitting manager. The experience almost ruined Joe.

Following a reorg, Joe was assigned to a new manager who was very different. Jerry looked for and gave endorsements to Joe when deserved, even when he just took small steps. Joe recounts the first time it happened, "One day, shortly after I was reassigned to Jerry, he came up to me and said, 'Joe, you have no idea how great your work is. Your pipeline report is excellent. In fact, I would like to share it with others as an example of what a completed form should look like. And what you shared at our team meeting earlier this week about sales calls was incredibly helpful to our team. Your sharing is more helpful than you can imagine. Thanks.'"

Joe continued, "You could have knocked me over with a feather when Jerry left the office that day, and I resolved to do anything I could for that man. Even though since then he has consistently given me positive, as well as some corrective, feedback, I will remember that first conversation the rest of my life."

Making It Real

Take this 24-hour challenge: In the next day, endorse at least five people, making sure that the endorsements are genuine, timely, and specific. Notice what happens, to you and to the other people!

PUTTING IT ALL TOGETHER

At this juncture, we have looked at a coaching process and some basic skills necessary to carry on a useful coaching conversation. As noted, these may seem simple, but they are not; a number of challenges can make the learning curve a steep one. And the biggest challenge may be time. Why?

- It takes time to slow down and be present and focused when people are speaking.
- It takes time to focus the conversation on what's most important.
- It takes time to ask questions to promote discovery and find out what the other person is thinking, rather than offering solutions or telling people what to do.
- It takes time to do a review instead of walking away from meetings, assuming everyone knows the next step.
- It takes time to give specific, timely and genuine endorsements for large as well as small accomplishments.

Making It Real

- What if you don't invest time in coaching others? It's entirely possible that one or two years from now, the same people will be asking the same questions and needing you in the same ways.
- What if you do invest time in coaching and developing others? It's entirely possible that you will be seen as someone who encourages others to think for themselves, who respects the ideas and thoughts of others, and who is considered innovative and efficient because individuals are allowed to arrive at solutions that are even better than those you have!

Which future do you prefer?

To summarize, it takes time to do all of these things well. But over the long term, the benefit of coaching is that people develop and become more and more self-reliant, with the result that managers and leaders can spend their time doing what they were hired for, not everyone else's jobs, too.

Taking Action

- Which segment of the coaching process is the most challenging for you? What will you do to practice and develop it?
- Which of the coaching skills do you need to develop further? With whom can you start practicing?
- With whom can you intentionally use coaching in the next week?

NOTES

1. Linda Miller, Madeleine Homan, and Scott Blanchard, *Coaching Essentials for Leaders*, a coaching skills training program offered through The Ken Blanchard Companies.
2. Ram Charan and Geoffrey Colvin. "Why CEOs Fail," *Fortune* Magazine (June 21, 1999): 78.
3. Ken Blanchard, Thad Lacinak, Chuck Thompkins, and Jim Ballard, *Whale Done: The Power of Positive Relationships*, (New York: The Free Press, 2002), 35.

CHAPTER 6

Coaching to Support Learning

ACTING ON BEST INTENTIONS

When Melanie found out she was being promoted to a management position in her company, she was immediately elated. Then, the reality hit. While technically competent, Melanie knew that she had no managerial experience. Worse, she had worked with very few good role models. "Not to worry," said her HR professional, "We will get you into Management 101 and you will learn the skills you need." Melanie should have been relieved. But she knew that Management 101 would be only the beginning of a steep learning curve.

While there are many ways that people learn, there are three types of learning involved in "acting on your best intentions" when it comes to moving up in your organization: on-the-job development, social learning, and training. These are illustrated in Figure 6.1 and defined in depth in the following subsections.

ON-THE-JOB DEVELOPMENT

Think about your own development at work. What helped you improve your performance most quickly? Was it a manager who gave you needed direction? A developmental project you took on to move the organization forward, an experience that stretched your skills? A manager who challenged you when you needed it? A coworker from whom you learned a great deal? Or, as in many companies in recent years, did you work with a coach,

	70% ON-THE-JOB DEVELOPMENT			20% SOCIAL LEARNING		10% TRAINING
	Coaching	Developmental Projects	Learning Through Observation	Mentor	Professional Groups/ Board Memberships/ Networking	Formal Training
Ask "what" and "how" questions	X			X		
Clarify and assess capabilities and preferences			X			X
Sharpen career direction	X			X		
Expand personal network of colleagues					X	
Hone skills		X			X	
Identify opportunities for growth	X			X		
Obtain specialized skills and knowledge				X		X
"Safe" practice of skills	X	X	X		X	X
Set development goals	X					

Figure 6.1

Three Types of Professional Development

whether internal or external to the company, who encouraged you to discover the best options and take effective action?

Approximately 70 percent of all development occurs "on the job." On-the-job development occurs in a number of ways, described here and illustrated in Figure 6.1.

- *Coaching.* Because coaching is focused on real work in real time, coaching is part of on-the-job development. A coach helps people think about a variety of aspects of their work experience. Examples of coaching as part of on-the-job development include identifying specific behaviors that need to be changed, setting SMART goals around projects, determining how to proceed in challenging situations, and seeing situations from a different perspective in order to move forward more smoothly.
- *Developmental projects.* Being able to identify specific projects or situations that can further the development of a person is a part of on-the-job development. For example, someone with limited experience might be asked to design a process for

improving a specific aspect of the business; another person might be asked to work on a cross-functional team focused on increasing customer satisfaction; still another person might be asked to define an agenda for an upcoming professional meeting. Each of these is an example of a project that is part of the job but is also used to develop specific skills for a certain individual.

- *Learning through observation.* Part of on-the-job development involves observing others who are already experienced at particular skills. Someone who is new to curriculum design, for example, might be asked to partner with an experienced designer in order to learn the process. Another individual who is learning how to design internal Web sites might be partnered with a veteran Web site designer to learn the skills and process involved. Senior consultants might take junior consultants on client visits to enable them to witness first-hand how projects are handled.

When developmental gaps or opportunities are identified, the key is to determine which job development activities will offer the best learning experience. For example, if you know you will be moving up in the company, think about how to get ready for the change. Be proactive. Plan ahead. Talk with your direct reports or your manager to identify potential developmental projects you can take on to prepare yourself. Find out whom you can observe, or ask to work with a coach. These on-the-job development activities result in a win-win-win environment for the company, the impending change or project, and for you.

SOCIAL LEARNING

Professional developmental opportunities also occur as a function of social interactions, just as they do in professional situations. Social interactions, which constitute about 20 percent of development opportunities, produce social learning. Two of these activities are mentoring and professional networking.

Mentoring

Mentoring is different from coaching in that a big part of what a mentor does is to share his or her wealth of knowledge and experience. In contrast, a coach might share small segments of personal experience, but the focus is on drawing out information from the person being coached. Coaching and mentoring, separately or together, can be a powerful way of developing others.

Mentoring relationships can be formed within the company where you work or with someone in a different firm. In the past few years, mentoring has been encouraged either formally or informally. Mentors help the person's development by talking about key milestones and projects or people who have been influential in their own development. The mentor also typically helps to surface anticipated challenges, obstacles, or politics within the organization or industry.

Networking

Social learning also takes place when you network professionally and join work-related groups or associations. Almost every aspect of the corporate world has a professional association. Many, such as the Society for Human Resource Management (www.shrm.org) and the American Society for Training and Development (www.astd.org), have local chapters throughout the country, and sponsor outstanding conferences featuring great speakers and networking events.

For executives specifically, there are such groups as Vistage, (formerly The Executive Committee; www.vistage.com), and the Conference Board (www.conferenceboard.org). Vistage offers executives and key leaders the chance to meet monthly with other leaders to discuss challenges and decision making in a confidential setting. The Conference Board holds regional meetings featuring excellent speakers and networking opportunities.

So, no matter what your field, take the time to discover which professional groups you can join to give you important networking opportunities. If none are available, create one! Many professionals have launched networks in their geographical areas by inviting friends in similar organizational positions to get together on a regular basis. They meet to share job openings, referrals, and pertinent resources. In many cases, members also become friends, offering one another support of a more personal nature.

TRAINING

Training today is a billion-dollar business, and is often the first place people look when they have developmental gaps they need to fill or want to learn new skills. A core belief may be that the classroom environment is the best place to learn, and learn to apply, specific content. Certainly, for some, that may be true, but most organization leaders would agree that the consistent application of training in the workplace does not always follow. In fact, training may contribute only about 10 percent to meeting developmental needs in organizations.

Traditionally, most training was conducted face to face in classes, but more organizations today are using different delivery approaches, including e-learning and virtual classrooms via teleconference technology. Others are using a blended approach, where participants experience several methods of content delivery.

In contrast, in the past 10 years, evidence has shown that training followed by coaching increases retention and application of learned skills in the workplace. In case studies where coaching

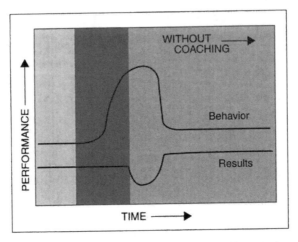

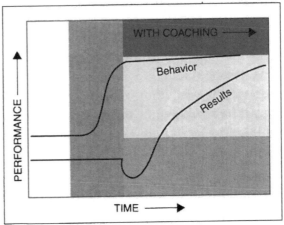

Figure 6.2
Training with and without Coaching[1]

was used to support training, productivity rose 88 percent, four times greater than the productivity increase experienced by those who were not coached. (See Figure 6.2.)

In a *Training and Development Journal* article entitled "The Coaching Controversy," author Neil Rackham states, "However excellent your classroom training, without good coaching you are probably wasting 87 cents out of every skills dollar you spend!"[1]

Making It Real

- Recall a time you had to learn something new, then ask yourself, what was most useful as you were in the development process?
- How you can use this information as you continue to develop in new areas?

What Is the Impact of Coaching When Coupled with Training?

Coaching creates a just-in-time learning environment. As few as three coaching sessions, over a six- to eight-week period, will keep the training content fresh in people's minds and serve as a subtle accounting of the application of new skills. During the coaching sessions, the focus is on using the new knowledge in the workplace, thereby leveraging the organization's training dollar. Thus, a training event becomes a learning process, as the coach encourages the application of skills in the work environment. As Joni Wickline, a senior coach with The Ken Blanchard Companies, has said, "Coaching helps people act on their own good intentions."

Unlike a training event, coaching is flexible. It consists of small increments of time (typically, 30 to 60 minutes per coaching conversation) that can accommodate a person's schedule. A minimum of three coaching sessions is recommended, and some organizations offer as many as 10 as a follow-up to training. Often, the people being coached appreciate the experience so much that they ask to extend their coaching sessions, so be prepared for this to come up!

One question that organizations often wrestle with is, "Who will provide the coaching?" In some companies, external coaches are preferred; for others, it's less expensive to free up time inside the organization to provide internal coaching. Either way, for best results, be sure that those doing the coaching know the training content.

At the beginning of each coaching conversation, whether internal or external, it's important to begin by establishing the focus. This can be done through precise questioning, one of the skills that coaches use to connect content with application for the person being coached. Some questions that a coach might ask:

- What areas of the training content caught your attention?
- What can you apply immediately from the training experience?
- What obstacles do you anticipate, and how will you overcome them?
- What was most challenging for you?
- Who can be a resource to you if you need additional support?

Coaching takes training to a deeper level, helping people break through any resistance they may have to implementing behavioral changes. In addition:

- *Coaching institutes accountability.* Training participants know that someone will be asking how they will be applying what they've learned in their day-to-day work.
- *Coaching is customized.* Obviously, each participant will have different needs. Coaching takes individual preferences into consideration and focuses on the individual's practical work situations and professional relationships.
- *Coaching enables a sustainable learning process.* Coaching transitions a training event into a learning process by keeping the content fresh in people's minds, through conversations that extend past the training.
- *Coaching ensures the training investment will pay off.* Participants actually experience and practice what they've learned

in the classroom in a safe environment. This allows them to discuss and practice the behavioral changes that were introduced in the training environment.

What Kind of Training Does Coaching Support?

Coaching can support any kind of training, at any level: the development of specific skills, leadership development, sales training, and others. In one organization, the leadership development process included three different modules presented by three different companies over the course of six months: one on values, one on leadership competencies, and one called Situational Leadership II. Coaching was provided to keep the emerging leaders moving forward as they applied the various training components and to help them understand how they fit together.

What Are the Main Challenges and Benefits of Coaching to Support Learning?

Over the past few years, coaching has become a standard way to follow up training in many companies. Through surveys and other data-gathering initiatives, a number of themes have emerged regarding both the challenges and benefits of using coaching to support learning.

Challenges
- *It's expensive.* True, it costs time and money to offer coaching. Organizations may pay up to several hundred dollars per coaching session, per person, even when conducted over the telephone. And follow-up coaching can take 30 to 60 minutes per call. Coaching costs in other ways, too, especially if it isn't used to support learning, as the return on training investment typically is low in this circumstance.

- *There's no time for coaching.* This is true, too. And, if time isn't allocated for follow-up coaching, it decreases the possibility that learned skills will be applied effectively and consistently in the workplace.
- *No one inside our company knows how to coach.* That may or may not be true. There are several options if this is a concern. Outside coaches can be brought in and trained on the necessary content. Likewise, HR professionals or OD specialists who are interested in coaching can be trained to provide coaching services. Finally, internal coaches can be identified and trained.

Benefits
- Improved focus on goal setting and goal achievement
- Application of training concepts on the job
- Increased implementation of training knowledge following the training event
- Expansion of skills and competencies
- Improved relationships with managers and direct reports
- Improved morale as development occurs
- Increased retention of key people

MEASURING SUCCESS

NOTE

Refer back to Chapter 4 for more on this topic.

Surveys and informal anecdotal data collection may be the most efficient and effective ways to gather data from coaching initiatives that follow training or learning events. Surveys can be brief and focused on highly specific information. They also can be useful in obtaining scaled information and anecdotal information.

Sample survey questions in this area may include:

- Now that some time has passed since your training took place, what from the experience has "stuck"?
- Overall, how would you rate your coaching experience?
  - Very satisfied
  - Satisfied
  - Neither satisfied nor dissatisfied
  - Dissatisfied
  - Very dissatisfied
- Specifically, what was most useful to you during the follow-up coaching sessions?
- Did you encounter obstacles during the coaching period? If so, what were they?
- Would you recommend coaching as a follow-up to other types of training? If not, what would make the coaching more useful?
- List three things you are doing differently as a result of training and/or coaching?

Regardless of how information is gathered, it is beneficial to obtain feedback on the coaching initiative. The feedback can be used at any time to show effectiveness and return on investment.

Making It Real

Looking back on training you have received, try to recall how much information you applied as a result, and how quickly.

- What might have been different if you had been reviewing the training content every few weeks with someone who was interested in how you were applying it on the job?
- What might you do in the future to apply the learning more quickly and effectively?

Taking Action

- What kind of follow-up procedure does your organization implement after training?
- Who can you influence to increase the probability that people will apply the training they received in the workplace?
- What, specifically, will you do to explore coaching to support learning in your organization?

NOTE

1. Neil Rackham, "The Coaching Controversy," *Training and Development Journal* (Vol. 2, 1997): 89–101.

CHAPTER 7

Coaching for Performance

Helen, a senior HR manager, was on the phone with Mark, a head coach with a global coaching services provider.

"We have an individual, Carla, who really needs some help," said Helen. Carla gets the results; her numbers are good. Yet she is harsh with her employees and consistently receives poor feedback from her whole group. She has really high turnover, but she can't understand that her people quit because of her. We need a coach who will help her see that she can get the same results using less vinegar and more honey."

"Hmmm," said Mark. "May I ask a few questions to understand the situation better?"

"Sure," said Helen.

"What feedback has Carla been given?"

"Well, her manager has repeatedly told her about the situation, and has asked for changes," explained Helen. "Carla's numbers are so great that it's hard to think about letting her go, but we are thinking that we may have to if she doesn't change her behavior."

"What are the consequences if Carla doesn't change her behavior?"

Helen took a moment to think. "I am not sure about that. Carla's manager is a little overwhelmed and hasn't really had much time to spend with her."

"Our experience with performance coaching," said Mark, "is that it works only when we set up a very clear series of events, which involve a fair amount of time and commitment on the part of the manager. Would you like to hear more about it?"

"Absolutely," said Helen, "that would be useful."

SETTING UP PERFORMANCE COACHING

Coaching for performance, or performance coaching, is coaching geared specifically to improving results or achieving higher performance. It can be a precarious proposition, however. Initially one of the primary uses for coaching, today performance coaching is considered by many to be too little, too late when used to correct a problematic employee. In fact, in many organizations, coaches are called in to do managers' jobs because the managers themselves are so overwhelmed by their own workloads they cannot possibly manage the performance of their direct reports.

Taking Preparatory Steps

Before a coach is called in to help with performance management, the manager and the employee should do the following:

1. Define the goals and tasks the manager expects the employee to complete. Special attention must be paid to describing the gap between what is needed/expected and what is currently being done.
2. Identify short-term milestones, if needed, to ensure goal completion in a timely manner.
3. Paint the picture of what a good job looks like for the employee, with a detailed description of activities and behaviors expected.
4. Explain in detail how the job should be done, with a clear description of which behaviors are unacceptable.
5. Spell out the consequences for noncompliance with all agreed-upon tasks and behaviors.

In regard to step 5, if the consequences are to be serious, such as job termination or loss of promotion, HR *must* be involved, and the performance plan must be in writing. If support and direction are needed to encourage the employee to learn and then apply new behaviors, a coach might be brought in to help guide detailed day-to-day behaviors, because often HR professionals and/or managers are either unable or unwilling to articulate the consequences. Instead, they tell the coach the consequences, and assume he or she will forward the message to the employee receiving the coaching. This approach is, needless to say, risky, as organizations generally end up with, at best, middling results or, at worst, legal consequences.

When there is a performance problem with an otherwise excellent employee, it rarely exists in a vacuum. Each employee's behavior is directly affected by the context of his or her boss and team.

But before sending in a coach to help, ask these questions:

- What, if any, feedback has the manager given the employee?
- Has the manager given the "hard" feedback?
- What is the evidence that the employee has heard and understood the feedback?
- Has the employee been given a clear to-do list?
- Has the employee been given a clear list of don'ts?
- Does the employee have the skills/capabilities needed to make the required change(s)?
- What does the manager need in order to provide appropriate direction and support to help the employee make the required changes?
- What are the specific skills that the employee needs to learn?
- Where/how is the employee going to learn those skills?
- Have the consequences for noncompliance been defined and communicated?
- How will the employee be expected to communicate progress in the situation to colleagues and direct reports?
- How can the employee's direct reports be part of the employee's growth and change process?
- How might the employee's direct reports and colleagues support the employee's behaviors and approaches?

GETTING BUY-IN

Often, when an employee who is struggling receives coaching, selected influential direct reports of that person might also benefit from coaching. This enables the coaches to help all stakeholders address their perceptions and change their attitudes, if need be. When many players have a coach, it increases the likelihood that the struggling employee will have an easier time identifying and taking responsibility for his or her part of the problem. Furthermore, the person identified as having behavior problems won't feel singled out and so will be much more likely to be open to change.

In organizations where coaching is used only to address performance problems, a difficult dynamic exists from the start, as it becomes challenging to position coaching as anything other than punitive. To address this dilemma, in many organizations, coaching is used for performance as well as development purposes. This way, people who are selected for coaching don't see themselves as problem employees; rather, they regard coaching as an investment in their potential. This approach goes a long way toward creating an environment that is conducive to openness and growth.

One danger the coach needs to watch out for, especially when a person is receiving performance coaching, is that the individual may tend to "yes" the coach and everyone else in the organization. He or she may feign understanding of the problem, discuss it in good faith with the coach, and may even do homework; and colleagues may even see some good changes. But as soon as the coaching is over, the individual reverts to old habits.

How can a coach know whether the person being coached is working in earnest? Unfortunately, it's impossible to be entirely sure. The key to a positive outcome, however, lies in setting up the coaching program carefully in the first place and making sure that the person being coached regards the undertaking as a privilege, not a punishment.

Making It Real

What steps can you take, if using performance coaching in your organization, to ensure that individuals being coached treat coaching as a privilege, not a punishment?

DELIVERING FEEDBACK

Giving feedback is an art, not a science. Entire shelves of books have been written on the subject, and it is beyond the scope of this book to discuss it at length here. We do, however, want to offer a few important guidelines for giving feedback, whether delivered by an HR professional, a manager, or a coach. These suggestions are based on coaching theory and technique, and can work well in any coaching situation. And for more in-depth coverage of this topic, we recommend the book *What Did You Say? The Art of Giving and Receiving Feedback*, by Charles N. Seashore, Edith Whitfield Seashore, and Gerald M. Weinberg.

1. The first step in giving feedback is to give *yourself* some well-considered feedback. Ask yourself questions in the following areas:
   - *Judgment/sanction.* What opinions or judgments do I have that might make me less objective?
   - *Need to be right.* Will giving feedback serve this person, the team, or the organization? Or will it serve my need to be right?
   - *True motives.* What is my real reason for giving this feedback? Am I really speaking for myself?
   - *Desire to "fix" another person.* What do I stand to gain from having this conversation? What do I stand to lose?

- *Credibility*. Do I have enough history, trust, and respect with this person to be credible?
- *Adequate preparation*. Am I ready to focus on specific behaviors and facts?

2. The next step is to ask the employee being coached if he or she is interested in hearing feedback. If the employee says, yes, that makes it easy. Nevertheless, be sure to establish the context for any feedback—for example, make it clear why the feedback might be important to the individual's success at work. If the employee says no, ask another question: "What is going on that you are not interested in hearing something that might be useful to you?"

3. If the feedback you're planning to give is of a particularly sensitive nature, first ask for permission, and explain that what you're about to say may make both of you uncomfortable. For example, you might say, "I'd like to share an observation that might make you uncomfortable. Is that acceptable to you?" Or, "I need to tell you something that might be hard to hear. Are you willing to listen?"

4. Give feedback directly, using as few words as possible and in as neutral a way as possible.

5. Know when to remain silent, to allow for thought. Resist the temptation to "fill the space" with lots of words.

6. Offer supporting evidence for your observations, if possible. Do not give more than three specific examples, however, as more than that will be overwhelming.

7. Refrain from making blanket statements that begin, "You always," or "You never," as this puts people on the defensive and will not produce the desired result. People on the defensive will attempt to distract from what they're being told, so be prepared to deflect these attempts and bring that person back to the feedback.

8. Listen and empathize. Just remember, empathy is not agreement.

9. Leave enough time for significant dialogue following the delivery of feedback.

Once you've delivered your feedback, there are a number of effective follow-up coaching questions you can ask, to "bring home" the insights you've offered:

- Do you agree that the feedback is accurate? What might be useful in it?
- How might you use this feedback to increase your effectiveness, improve your relationships, or achieve your goal?
- What actions are you willing to take based on this feedback?

You also need to do follow-up on yourself. Ask:

- Did I say everything that needed to be said? If not, how/when will I complete the conversation?
- How should I follow up with this person later?
- Have I been clear about my commitments to this person?
- What might I do further to help/serve this person?

MAKING CHANGES

Some performance problems stem from an attitude or belief regarding organizational expectations that a coach can help to change. Often, perceived performance problems are simply the result of a disconnect between the individual's style and that of his or her boss and/or colleagues. Obviously, each individual brings to the organization distinct cultural and professional habits and strong personality traits. Coaches can help employees "fit in" and generate clarity about such organizational expectations as:

- *Deliverables.* Employees need explicit directions as to what is expected, by when, in what format.
- *Deadlines.* Some people come from cultures that regard deadlines as guidelines rather than hard-and-fast rules. The manager must establish what is the case in the organization's culture.

- *Group norms.* For example, tell new employees, "We don't use email chains here."
- *Behaviors.* For example, tell new employees, "We don't blame others. We notice problems and talk about how to fix them."

Making It Real

What are some group norms in your organization that should be communicated to all new employees?

Other performance problems stem from habits that people have developed over time to help them to be successful in a specific role, but are now derailing that person who has taken on a new position. A classic example is when a person whose previous success has depended on his or her individual achievements is promoted to manager and has no idea how to delegate to accomplish assignments.

Unfortunately, habits are notoriously hard to break. Fortunately, coaches are exceptionally good at helping people do just that. Coaches, whether external or internal (or managers using coaching skills), must be able to help people think through how they will implement the three most important and closely linked tools for breaking an undesirable habit: structure, accountability, and support (see Figure 7.1).

Structure: Identifying and using systems and tools (e.g., a calendar, a to-do list, etc.) to be more effective. To develop a solid structure to change behavior, coaches can ask the person being coached to identify how and when the bad habit(s) emerged, and discuss which systems or tools might help establish new behaviors.

Accountability: Including others to ensure follow-through. The person being coached should inform key stakeholders

Figure 7.1
Formula for Action

about new personal habits and ask for accountability checks. One manager told his direct reports that he was learning and practicing to be a better listener and asked them to use a simple hand signal when they noticed him interrupting. The manager's team was delighted to be included and thrilled to be given a way to stop the interruptions. The manager was shocked to discover just how deeply ingrained this habit was. Other accountability tools include daily reminders or checklists that can be completed at day's end.

Support: Accessing and leveraging all available resources to get the job done. Everyone needs extra support to accomplish difficult tasks. The key for the coach is to assess what that support looks like to the individual being coached, and in consideration of that person's situation. Keep in mind, one person's cheerleader is another person's annoyance. The person being coached must think about what has worked in the past and what good support would be currently. Then the person must be coached to seek those who can provide that support.

Performance coaching can work well when the HR leader and the manager of the person being coached are willing to tell the truth as they see it, but without blame or judgment. They must also be decisive and courageous about the consequences if the person being coached fails to change his or her undesirable behaviors.

Taking Action

- How, specifically, might coaching for performance be helpful in your organization?
- How will you ensure that the coaching is communicated as an investment in the person being coached?
- What specific steps will you take to implement coaching for performance in your organization?

NOTE

1. Charles N. Seashore, Edith Whitfield Seashore, and Gerald M. Weinberg, *The Art of Giving and Receiving Feedback*, Bingham House Books, 1992.

CHAPTER 8

Coaching for Leadership Development

David is a 38-year-old midlevel manager, rising through the ranks of a large discount retail company. The company is growing rapidly, and he knows the executive ranks will be expanding. David is clear that he wants to become regional VP, but he wonders if he'll be given a shot at a promotion. He knows he has the tenure and the in-depth knowledge of the business, and that he's done his job well and is viewed as an asset. But along the way he's had run-ins with a few colleagues who haven't always viewed him favorably.

Last week, just as he was set to return one of the many calls he gets from search firms, he got a call from his manager's boss. David learned that the company was considering him for a new position, but that the promotion was contingent upon his working with a coach.

He doesn't know much about coaching, and certainly hasn't experienced it, but he's open to new possibilities and ways of learning. In any case, he figures he has nothing to lose, and much to gain. So he scheduled the coaching call and then began to learn what he could about working with a coach, as preparation for the first meeting.

THE LEADERSHIP JOURNEY

When people join companies, especially young employees trained in specific skills, they usually start as individual contributors. They are assigned specific key responsibility areas directly linked to their area(s) of expertise. They may be part of a team, but contribute as individuals. Figure 8.1 shows that Tom

135

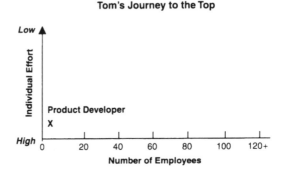

Figure 8.1
Leadership Effects of Coaching: No Direct Reports

came into the company as a product developer. His job was to, first, determine which new products were needed and, then, to help develop them. Although he worked with the marketing and sales department, he was an individual contributor with no direct reports.

As individual contributors grow and develop, they frequently are promoted into management roles. Often, however, they have no management experience and limited interpersonal skills, especially if their fields are highly technical.

In Tom's case (see Figure 8.2), after he was promoted into management and his number of direct reports increased, he had to

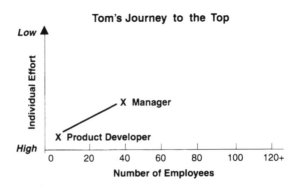

Figure 8.2
Leadership Effects of Coaching: Promoted into Management

Tom's Journey to the Top

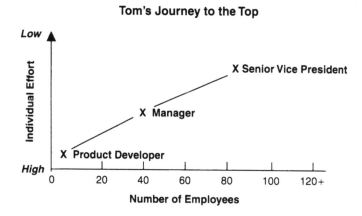

Figure 8.3

Leadership Effects of Coaching: Promoted to Senior Vice President

learn to delegate work, rather than do it himself as he was used to when he was an individual contributor.

Tom excelled once again! The company was so impressed with his management skills and abilities that he was promoted to senior vice president (see Figure 8.3), again with new responsibilities. At this level, he no longer did much individual contributing at all; rather, he set the strategic direction for an entire division.

Leaders at this level in the organization are responsible for delegating most of the individual work to others. As senior VP, Tom had 80 people reporting either directly to him or to his direct reports, and his division was responsible for $35 million in revenues.

Over time, Tom was promoted yet again, to the very top: CEO. At that level in organizations, leaders are fully responsible for helping to establish, and then uphold, the company's vision, values, and mission. They must focus on strategy and building a leadership team, network with other CEOs, and recognize quickly what is working and what is not and how to fix it!

In Tom's case (see Figure 8.4), the technical skills that had served him so well early in his career were a thing of the past. As the top-level executive, he now had to delegate all individual

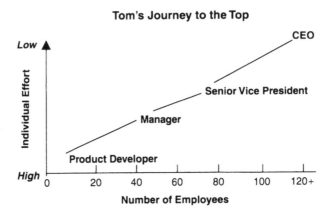

Figure 8.4

Leadership Effects of Coaching: Promotion to CEO

tasks, for his primary role was to oversee the entire company's success or failure. This level of responsibility is what sets executives apart from other employees in the organization. Executives are charged with leading others to excellence so that the entire organization succeeds. If they try to do too much themselves, progress will stall. They must be willing and able to work through others.

EXECUTIVE COACHING

WHAT IT IS, WHAT IT'S NOT

One of the earliest forms of coaching, executive coaching today is regarded as an investment by an organization in its senior leaders. Executives themselves embraced coaching as a learning tool for themselves well before it became widely used with teams, middle management, and other employees. This may have been because coaching was a new concept or because business leaders thought it would pay off best at higher levels, or simply because they wanted to try it on their leadership team before implementing it on a wider basis. Some organizations may have delved into coaching because it was new and different and the buzzword for a rapidly growing trend, or because a competitor had tried it and

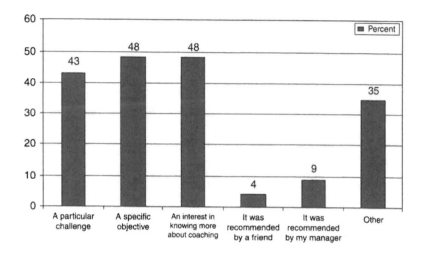

Figure 8.5
Reasons for Working with an Executive Coach

was clearly benefiting from it. For these and other reasons, traditionally coaching was introduced into organizations through executives, who were early adopters of the practice.

Executives by their nature are high-functioning, competent, motivated people who have earned their positions because of their strengths and skills. Executive coaching can galvanize their growth trajectory in the right direction, increasing personal and organizational success.

WHAT EXECUTIVES NEED—AND DON'T NEED—FROM COACHES

In 2005, The Ken Blanchard Companies conducted a survey with leaders who had received coaching in the previous few years. The survey was intended to discover the reasons for hiring a coach and the expectations for working with a coach. The top three reasons (see Figure 8.5) survey respondents cited for hiring a coach were:

1. They had a specific objective that they wanted to focus on.
2. They were interested in knowing more about coaching.
3. They were facing a particular challenge.

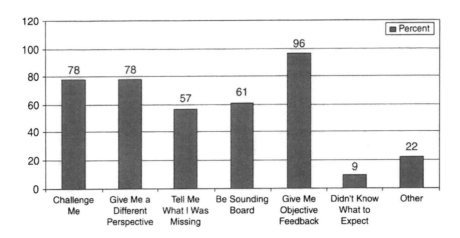

Figure 8.6
Executive Expectations of Coach

Survey participants also were asked to describe expectations they had of the coach during the coaching process. The number-one answer was that they wanted to receive objective feedback. As shown in Figure 8.6, other responses were:

1. To challenge me.
2. To give me a different perspective.
3. To serve as a sounding board.
4. To tell me what I was missing [as an executive].

TIP

Use executive coaching to:

- Serve as a springboard for new thinking and better decision-making processes.
- Help executives set new directions.
- Identify goals and objectives.

FLOW OF LEADERSHIP DEVELOPMENT AND EXECUTIVE COACHING

In the past, developing leadership capability was done on the job. Wisdom came, at least in theory, over time—although often employees moved into leadership positions simply as a function of seniority. Those days are gone. Young people today are being thrust into leadership positions that require wisdom and maturity far beyond what one could expect from them, given their age and experience levels. Typically, they are fast-tracked for leadership positions because they show specific competencies that their organizations need *now,* and because rapid growth is forcing these companies to rely on the much younger and more inexperienced workforce. This situation will only escalate as the 85 million baby boomers begin to retire and are replaced by a much smaller and younger workforce.

Fortunately, the young are stepping up to the challenge. But they need help, and many are getting it in the form of leadership development coaching. The clear fact is, developing leaders and executives, no matter what their age, can benefit from a strong coaching relationship.

NOTE

The remainder of this chapter will use the terms *leadership development* and *executive coaching* interchangeably. The term *leader* will be used to refer both to those who are developing into higher positions of leadership as well as executives who are engaged in the coaching process.

BEFORE EXECUTIVE COACHING BEGINS

Coaching, as we defined earlier, is an intentional process leading to intentional action and change (refer back to Chapter 2 for a description of the general process of coaching). But there are some specific differences between coaching for the flow of leadership development and executive coaching. In any coaching relationship, however, to ensure a more satisfying and productive coaching process for all involved, it's always a good idea to start with a detailed agreement detailing how the executive coaching process will proceed.

It's also essential before coaching begins to define and share the communications protocol with all participants. To instill trust between the coach and executive, the executive must be confident that anything said during a coaching session will be kept confidential. Establishing communication agreements ensures that everyone understands who will talk with whom, about what, and when. Expanded communication within the organization is encouraged between the person being coached and other senior leaders, colleagues, or team members, but it is the responsibility of the person being coached to share feedback about the process and the coaching conversations to his or her manager, HR professional, and/or others who need to be kept informed. To that end, it is useful, prior to the start of coaching, to set up a conference call involving the person to be coached, his or her manager and/or an HR representative, and the coach. The purpose of the meeting is to discuss what will occur during the coaching; clarify goals and objectives for the organization; and address confidentiality issues, the coaching agreement, and expected results from the coaching.

The organization, of course, has a right to be involved in setting objectives for coaching and desired end results. These typically will align with the organization's competencies and strategies. Examples of objectives include increasing levels of communication among team members, improving retention of key employees by a certain percentage, identifying specific sales data or targets, and increasing leadership effectiveness as evidenced by a particular promotion. Focusing on these areas as part of the agreement process before coaching begins ensures that the coach and leader are starting "on the same page."

Executive Coaching in Progress

Once the coaching is under way, the leader often benefits from *shadow coaching*, whereby the coach observes the leader in his or her day-to-day activities and gives immediate feedback. Shadow coaching may include observing the person leading a meeting, conducting one-on-one interactions with subordinates, or generally relating to peers or superiors in the organization.

Executive and leadership development coaching can take anywhere from six months to a year or more, depending on the leader's commitment and motivation and his or her goals and objectives. A coachable leader typically has in mind achieving one or more of the following: sustainable changes, increased awareness, insight from assessments, and long-term behavioral changes. Bear in mind, however, that during the coaching sessions, some of the initial objectives may change, which is a common occurrence. Executives and leaders are encouraged to communicate this information with their senior executives, HR professionals, and/or others who may need to know.

At the Conclusion of Executive Coaching

As the executive coaching process draws to a close, the leader and coach will begin a debriefing process, to bring the learning to completion and to review with the leader his or her new knowledge, in order to sustain success. Together, the coach and leader will determine next steps that will continue to move the leader and the organization forward. Achieving good closure leads to sustained success, a distinctive mark of effective coaching.

NOTE

Leadership development, or executive coaching, is rarely used to address problematic behavior. Although leaders may seek to adjust their behavior through coaching, this process is not intended as a punitive measure. And if the leader perceives it as such, early resistance may block any benefits and learning that would otherwise be possible from the relationship.

Making It Real

In light of your organization's need for future leaders, is enough emphasis being put on long-term development of emerging leaders and on goals and results?

USE OF ASSESSMENTS IN EXECUTIVE COACHING

Coaching certainly does not depend on assessments, but they can be valuable tools in the coaching process. If they are to be used, the executive coach will want to identify the assessments currently being used in the organization, which may be:

- 360s and other assessments for leadership competencies
- Myers-Briggs Type Indicator,[1] DiSC Profile,[2] and other personality inventories
- EQ[3] mapping for leadership or executive competencies

By identifying current assessment tools in use, a coach can then incorporate them into the learning process. And by working with the organizational contact or the leader, the coach can decide whether additional assessment tools are needed in the coaching process. Assessment issues to consider:

- Which assessment tools does your organization currently use, or do you anticipate it needing?

- If you know you'll be expanding use of assessments, how can you leverage and use the information to most effectively influence the individuals being coached, as well as the organization?

FOCUS AREAS FOR LEADERSHIP DEVELOPMENT COACHING

Organizational leaders, and especially executives, are charged with making an impact and influencing others. The executive coach's overriding goal is to ensure their impact and influence will be positive. The leader's job is to accomplish goals in a unique and personal way, working through other people to shape an organization. Leaders, of course, are as diverse as any other group of people. One may be hard-hitting, another subdued; a third may be decisive, a fourth more collaborative in nature. Each has his or her own performance style, and uses it to make a company successful.

> One executive had a run-in with a peer in another area of the organization. And though she knew her behavior was out of line, she said, "I am who I am. I expect you to learn to accommodate my personality and to work with me." However, she made no similar allowances for others.

Needless to say, there are leaders like the one just described who don't want, or see the need, to change or improve their professional behavior. Like this woman, they believe that because they're at the top of the organizational hierarchy, everything and everyone should revolve around her. As in this example, resistance to change isn't usually about learning a new skill—for example, an innovative technology. More often it centers on "people issues"—working with a team, learning to delegate effectively, being receptive to ideas from subordinates, improving communication, and so on. For leaders with the "won't change" mind-set, coaching can help them reevaluate their people skills, styles, and commitment levels in order to find more effective ways to function in their roles.

STRATEGIC AND OPERATIONAL LEADERSHIP

Leadership can be divided into two main categories: strategic and operational. This theory has emerged from a body of research and meta-analysis of research[4] undertaken to identify the what and how of leadership. Coaching can help leaders assess both their strategic and operational abilities for the purpose of identifying gaps and strengthening areas in which they are weak.

Strategic Leadership

Aspects of strategic leadership include vision, culture, and strategic imperatives. Thus, coaches who work with leaders to strategize more effectively focus on:

1. Articulating the organization's vision to ensure that everyone in the company is working toward the same goals. The vision should never be something that is announced, then hung on a plaque somewhere and virtually ignored. The job of the strategic leader is to keep the company "eye on the prize."
2. Defining and building the culture. The strategic leader defines the culture of an organization, according to company values, priorities, expectations, and goals and objectives. Based on the company culture, lower-level managers then create team cultures within that larger environment.
3. Setting strategic imperatives for any given time period. The leader ensures that all resources are deployed for the purpose of achieving company goals to achieve the established strategic imperatives. He or she carefully monitors deployment and behaviors, curtailing any that are off-purpose.

Operational Leadership

Aspects of operational leadership include management practices that drive policies, procedures, and systems. Leaders at the operational level are responsible for strategy as well as operations. Coaching can help these leaders:

1. Understand their group dynamic so that they may set effective policies. Once a policy has been set, operational leaders are then charged with assuring, in a reasonable manner, that it is followed.
2. Establish procedures for communicating, making decisions, managing conflict, responding to emergencies, and solving problems. Operational leaders help the group determine norms and roles and then function within them.
3. Create clear and elegant systems that make it easy for people to do their jobs, for others in the company to interact with their team, and, overall, make the company customer-friendly.

Is it any wonder developing leaders need coaches? A new leader is required to have an analytical mind and an excellent memory; to be creative; to have a passion for work; and to be self-disciplined. It is, simply, a fiendishly difficult job to be the leader of others. No one can do it well all the time. That's why most companies form leadership teams whose members have complementary strengths.

CHARACTER AND INTEGRITY

Character and integrity are critical qualities of all leaders at every level of the organizational hierarchy. Without them, no leader can succeed for long. The research is unequivocal on this, and recent events have proven it out. Leaders lacking character and/or integrity may function seemingly successfully for some time;

but, eventually, their weaknesses will manifest, causing not just personal failure but often that of their companies, as well.

Character and integrity are, however, difficult traits to define. We all receive lessons in these traits as we grow, from our parents, teachers, peers, sports coaches, and/or religious influences. But, ultimately, we each must define our own characters and sense of integrity. All leaders are stronger when they understand themselves and what leadership means in the framework of "self."

Making It Real

- What is your definition of character and integrity?
- How do you demonstrate them on a personal and professional basis?
- How similar is your view of yourself to that of others?

ON-BOARDING

On-boarding is a term used to describe the process by which key leaders move from one position to another. How effectively and quickly this happens depends on the individual and the situation, but usually it takes at least 90 days.

Much of the focus of on-boarding is on critical networking, essential resources, and a vision and strategy for their position that aligns with the company vision, mission, and goals.

To on-board successfully, leaders must be able to "read the landscape," to identify who can help them succeed, who they can trust, who are key influencers, and who can guide them through key processes. Getting to know these people and developing strong working relationships with them is critical when moving within an organization.

Understandably, then, on-boarding is a major focus area of executive coaching. Leaders work with their coaches to, first, identify and, second, assess the needed networks, then to evaluate their own first impressions.

On-boarding also means finding the "land mines"—that is, figuring out what is in danger of "blowing up" and determining how to keep that from happening. Thus, coaching high-level leaders often requires learning how to deal with red-flag issues without causing controversy, gaining some early and notable successes, and, possibly, delaying decisions around issues that don't have easy answers or that require deeper investigation.

Patty, a high-performing district manager in the sales division, received a voice message from Norm, her boss, asking her to schedule a meeting with him as soon as possible. She scheduled the meeting for later in the week. When she arrived in Norm's office, he told Patty that as a result of how well she had done at a district level, and in recognition of her excellent numbers, the company was planning to promote her to regional manager. The promotion would take effect in the next quarter. As part of the promotion process, Patty would be required to work with a coach who specialized in helping key employees make the move into higher-level positions.

With a coach's help, Patty was able to:

- Identify the knowledge she would need to succeed in her new role.
- Learn how to delegate work to others.
- Begin networking to develop relationships with key leaders at her new level in the organization
- Develop transition and implementation plans.
- Begin to plan positive behavioral changes she could make as she undertook the new role.
- Select additional training she would need in specific skill areas—leadership development, team relationships, and so on—to help her increase her effectiveness as a leader.

With her coach's help, Patty made a smooth and successful transition to the regional manager role. Her confidence led to greater trust and better working relationships among her team members and with other regional managers. She became an even greater asset to her company because of the leadership development coaching she received.

TIP

An excellent on-boarding resource is Michael Watkin's *The First 90 Days: Critical Success Strategies for New Leaders at All Levels* (Harvard Business School, 2003). This book guides newly positioned leaders to gain confidence in newly acquired roles and responsibilities.

By working with a coach during the on-boarding process, leaders can more quickly: identify strengths and skills they will need, determine how to employ or acquire those skills, understand the culture and corporate values from a new perspective, learn to work strategically, develop keen observation skills, evaluate assumptions, decide who to trust, and become aware of their own biases (and when they are in play). Making smooth transitions helps not only the leaders, but the organization as well.

Making It Real

- How does your organization help people transition from one position to another?
- How effective is your company's on-boarding process?
- What more can be done to help developing leaders ramp up more quickly?

Networking

When organizational leaders are in transition, whether moving from one level or division to another, they need to identify critical networks and develop an intentional plan to form new relationships with key people, if they are to succeed in their new roles.

Bill was being considered for a senior leader position at his company in the high-tech industry. Unfortunately, he had a bad relationship with Connor, one of the executives, caused years earlier when Bill had offended Connor and never dealt with it. Now Connor was blocking Bill's promotion.

Fortunately, Bill was invited to work with an executive coach, and he brought up the situation with Connor in one of the early coaching calls. Working with Barb, his coach, Bill acknowledged that something had to be done to address the old conflict if he was to move ahead successfully in the company. Moreover, he realized that it was in everyone's best interest—certainly his own!—to repair the relationship with Connor. To succeed at a higher level, Bill knew he would need a strong relationship with everyone on the senior leadership team, including Connor. But Bill worried that the relationship might be beyond repair. He and Barb continued to talk about it and, eventually, Bill decided to take the risk and try to repair the damage.

Barb asked Bill to describe the actions he was ready and willing to make. Bill said he'd contact Connor; following the coaching session, he made an appointment with Connor to discuss their differences. At the meeting, he accepted responsibility for the conflict. Then Connor admitted that he, too, shared the blame by allowing the conflict to remain unresolved for so long.

Ultimately, Bill was pleasantly surprised to find that his former adversary had become his greatest advocate, championing his promotion and helping him develop relationships with the other executives.

Make no mistake, however, not all stories end as happily as Bill's. Sometimes nothing will change another person's mind. But as Bill learned from his coaching, it is always best to be proactive in addressing bad situations caused by misunderstandings or bad behavior. Identifying relationships that need to be repaired or expanded, and then developing a strategic plan to work on them, are essential steps in the executive coaching process, particularly during on-boarding and other transitional periods.

Making It Real

- What relationships do you need to develop or repair?
- Who do you know that would be beneficial to connect with?
- When will you schedule the meeting(s)?

ASSUMPTIONS AND LIMITING BELIEFS

It is not uncommon for people to be unaware of assumptions or limiting beliefs they have that hold them back professionally. Leaders are no exception. And when brought to their attention, their initial response often is to become defensive or attempt to justify the assumptions or beliefs that are causing them professional problems.

For example, a leader might assume his or her employees are not capable of making good decisions, and so tend to micromanage to make sure the "right" decisions are being made in the department. The inability to partner with others, or the desire to remain a "lone ranger," may be rooted in this assumption. An effective executive coach will bring this misguided assumption to the leader's attention, and then help him or her to explore the beliefs underlying it, with the goal of replacing it with one more useful.

Another common mistake leaders make is to assume they know how far along their employees are in their work, and assign more (or fewer) tasks based on that "knowledge," causing misalignment of staff responsibilities.

Many leaders also assume that their employees need constant oversight, when in fact they're fully competent and would work more effectively without their boss "standing over their shoulder."

More dangerous limiting beliefs may be toward women, minorities, and/or subordinates, as these may have legal consequences for the leader and his or her organization.

Executive coaching can help leaders recognize these and other faulty assumptions or beliefs that are limiting their effectiveness.

Lacy, an executive in the automotive industry, was talking with Ben, a 30-year manager who had worked with her for many years. Ben came to Lacy asking for help in dealing with a challenging employee. Because Lacy knew Ben so well, she made the assumption that because of his years of experience, he already knew how to handle the situation. So, instead of giving Ben direction, Lacy casually asked him what he intended to do about it. In reality, this was a new dilemma for Ben, and he did not feel equipped to handle it. So Ben left Lacy's office frustrated. When Lacy later talked with her executive coach about the "disconnect" between her and Ben, the coach was able to help Lacy become more aware of her assumptions and how they impacted her behaviors.

Camille, a senior vice president in her company's marketing department, had a different leadership problem. She wanted Sean, one of her managers, to take a different approach to a challenging situation, so during a progress report Sean was giving to Camille, she interrupted and began giving detailed directions on what he should be doing differently. When Sean left, Camille knew something was wrong but had no idea what it was. Later that day, Camille shared what had happened with her executive coach, who helped her see that her beliefs about Sean's competence had led her to micromanage him and that such a tendency would be hurtful not just to Sean but to other members of her teams, who would come, rightly, to think that Camille had no confidence in them.

Clearly, assumptions and limiting beliefs get in the way of effective leadership. And they affect not only the organization but also employees' families, vendors, clients, and anyone else coming in contact with the organization.

To prevent such beliefs from taking hold, leaders need to ask themselves, "Do these people work for or with me? Do they work to serve me, or do I serve them so that they can do their job effectively?" As Scott Blanchard often says when speaking about the impact leaders have on others, "When you are the manager or leader, you are the dinner table conversation for those who work for you."

An effective executive coach will challenge faulty assumptions and beliefs so that leaders can shift into new beliefs and behaviors that better serve themselves and the organization. Coaching provides a safe environment for doing just that.

BLIND SPOTS

Like faulty assumptions and limiting beliefs, we all have blind spots about our behavior, things we do but are unaware of—whether a distracting mannerism (rattling change in the pocket), language we use (a phrase we repeat over and over), a distinctive habit (constantly tapping a pen or our foot when we talk), and myriad other behaviors. Though we may be blind to them, they are all too obvious to those around us. In executive leaders, these often-small, unrecognized behaviors can have surprisingly large consequences—limiting upward mobility, reducing company and team effectiveness, and lowering productivity.

> Larry, an executive coach, agreed to work on-site with Brandon, a senior VP, to do some shadow coaching. At the first meeting, several direct reports were in the room and others were attending via telephone conferencing. After the meeting, Larry casually asked Brandon what his perception was of Tim, one of the people on the telephone. Brandon responded, "Tim's contribution is minimal. He's still with the team, but barely." Larry then pointed out that every time Tim spoke up during the meeting, Brandon had rolled his eyes. Brandon acknowledged he had no idea he had done that. Larry then speculated as to the implications of this behavior, which was obvious to others in the room.

Just as in dealing with assumptions and limiting beliefs, leaders need to become aware of their blind spots, and coaching can help them become aware of any behaviors that are impeding their effectiveness, and may be hurting the team.

Making It Real

- How can you identify your limiting beliefs, assumptions, or blind spots?
- Which ones, if addressed, would help you to be more effective in your role?
- How will you address them?

STRENGTHENING LEADERSHIP CAPACITY

High-level leaders need to have a keen self-awareness, to know their strengths as well as their weaknesses. They also need to fully comprehend the organization's leadership competencies and align with them. Assessments such as 360s can be used to clarify what is strong, neutral, or needs to be changed in order for a leader to succeed.

For an executive coach, "strengthening capacity" means aligning with organizational goals and competencies and taking time to recognize gaps in order to strategically focus the executive coaching sessions, because filling in these gaps and overcoming liabilities will enable the executive to maximize his or her value and improve the potential for future growth, both personally and professionally.

> In one organization, a senior manager who was regarded as a strategic thinker, and was seen as an emerging leader positioned to move up in the organization, had the reputation for leaving people devastated after their encounters with him. Therefore, his company decided to offer him executive coaching to improve his relationship skills, thus preparing him for his future in the company.

Knowing whether a leader is willing and ready to make necessary changes is vital to all involved in any coaching initiative. The organization has to let its leaders know that resisting change will limit their careers. They also need to be made aware that

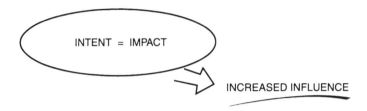

Figure 8.7
Aligning Intent with Impact

change does not necessarily mean a complete reworking. Even small, strategic adjustments can make a significant difference, and change the perception others have about them.

For example, executives need to become aware of the impression they make just by walking into the room. Do they come across as aggressive? Assertive? Confident? Communicative? Withdrawn? Angry? Engaging?

Perhaps you've seen the television ad that depicts an employee's perspective of different kinds of bosses—overbearing, funny, even sweaty. Then the employee *becomes* the boss, and has to decide which kind he will be. Every real-life executive has the same decision to make.

Once executives realize how others see them, they can begin to reshape their behavior to change that perception, if that's what's called for. Coaching can help executives be intentional about this effort, and vigilant about the impact they make. When there is strong alignment of intent with impact, it increases the leader's ability to influence and manage (see Figure 8.7).

In *Leverage Your Best, Ditch the Rest: The Coaching Secrets Top Executives Depend On* (HarperCollins, 2004), authors Scott Blanchard and Madeleine Homan urge executives to ask themselves these important questions:

- How do you see yourself?
- How do others see you?
- How do you want to be seen?
- Now what?

Being committed to learning and growing is the mark of successful and respected executives, who set the example for others to follow. This level of achievement can be aided by executive coaching, which addresses the critical leadership issues discussed in the following subsections.

STAYING MOTIVATED

Leaders don't always know what motivates them. In coaching, they find a safe place in which to explore and understand what it is that ignites their passion and energy, and to discover how to keep their motivation level high.

Some organizations are reluctant to address with their leaders problems of motivation or job performance because they worry that doing so will cause leaders to leave. In fact, changing jobs or moving to a new position isn't always what's needed. Rather, with the benefit of coaching, leaders may discover that all that is needed to do their job well is more education or training, or that another minor change will make a world of difference. And for those leaders who do realize that they want to be in another position, coaching can help them get into the right one. And when the right people are in the right positions, this ultimately helps the organization as well.

MAINTAINING CONFIDENCE

How confident is the leader? How does his or her confidence level reflect in job performance? What is the impact of the executive's confidence level on others? Many executives have such a high level of confidence it borders on arrogance. Others have such a low sense of self-confidence their behavior borders on self-effacement.

In *Good to Great: Why Some Companies Make the Leap and Others Don't*, author Jim Collins writes about "level-five leaders," those who demonstrate a rare combination of two traits: fierce and focused resolve combined with humility.[5] To describe this, he uses an illustration of a window and a mirror. When everything is going well, the level-five leader looks out the window and assigns success to others—an employee, a peer, a client, or even a competitor. When things are going badly, that same leader looks in the mirror and takes full responsibility for it. A poor leader does this in reverse—taking credit for the good and blaming others for the bad.

Having an appropriate level of confidence means being able to be humble and to give credit to others who are doing well. Confident leaders take praise graciously—they don't have to brandish their accomplishments; and they have no trouble taking responsibility. They address problems when/as they occur. Coaching can be highly effective in moving executives to level-five leadership.

ALIGNING WITH PRIORITIES

One issue that often arises when executives work with coaches is the life/work balance—that is, how to juggle their personal and professional priorities. Certainly, achieving true balance in life is difficult; nevertheless, an executive can learn to commit to making room for self, family, and recreation in his or her busy work life. Such a goal may be a critical part of what an executive wants to achieve through the coaching process.

Most executives need clarity about their priorities in life. They frequently spend 80 to 100 hours in the office every week, putting work ahead of everything else, and failing to acknowledge the impact doing so has on family and friends. By helping executives to clarify their priorities, coaching can make a big difference in an executive's health and happiness.

Coaches can ask leaders guiding questions to help them achieve this critical work/life balance:

- Where does your family fit in with your work?
- How do you take care of your personal health?

- How do you feed your spiritual self?
- In what ways do your calendar and schedule reflect your priorities?
- What actions can you take to help you align your personal and professional priorities?
- What in your work can you minimize, eliminate, or delegate?
- Which of your habits do you need to alter or encourage? Which new habits do you need to acquire?
- What are you communicating to others by working the large number of hours that you do?

It is not the goal of this effort to take the executive away from his or her work—especially if that work is important and fulfilling to the individual. The goal is for the executive to align his or her priorities, and to learn to work smarter by working through others. When executives see that doing so not only enables them to find greater balance in life but also is an investment in the future success of their organization, they are more likely to embrace a change in time management.

CHOOSING THE RIGHT TIME FOR COACHING

It is important that leaders receive coaching at the right time, the strategic time, for them. Coaching may be appropriate when they are promoted to a new position, when they feel stuck, or when the organization itself is changing. Or perhaps a leader realizes that he or she needs to make personal changes in order to be considered eligible for a larger role and level of influence in the company. Regardless of the focus, finding the appropriate time to begin coaching is essential.

Put another way, a leader must be ready for coaching. If a leader doesn't want to be coached or doesn't see the need for it, it will be a waste of everyone's time, as well as the organization's money. On the other hand, the coaching process can speed growth and development significantly when the leader is ready to maximize the potential of a successful coaching experience. Simply, if the leader doesn't "buy in," the coaching process won't work. If coaching is perceived as imposed, rather than as an investment in development, both the coach and the leader will be frustrated. In such cases, it's better to cease than to continue in a futile process.

It's also important to consider whether the leader is in the right environment for coaching, and whether he or she is properly matched with the coach. Keep in mind, too, that other things may be going on in the leader's life that block his or her focus on growth. Any number of reasons may distract the leader from being fully committed to the coaching process. Put simply, if the timing's not right, there's no point in proceeding.

To succeed with coaching, a leader must buy into the process. Committing to relying on the coach's expertise is the first step. To do this, the leader has to believe the coach is credible and that the time spent in coaching will make a difference. The leader also has to want to change, to grow.

> One leader, when offered the opportunity to work with a coach, declined, saying: "I know how I'm perceived, and that often it isn't good. I'm not the most popular person in the organization. But this isn't a beauty contest. Who I am has landed me where I am. I'm not interested in changing. I'll stick with who I am."

This leader was being honest. Sometimes a person who is reluctant to try coaching may be encouraged to do so if he or she clearly understands the consequences of not giving it a chance. Another approach is to ask other leaders who have benefited from being coached to share their experiences, as a way of opening the door for the reluctant leader. Or if the timing is wrong, it may be possible to raise the issue again in a few weeks. In the end, however, if the leader is just not willing to be coached, it is better to know this from the get-go than to force coaching on someone for whom it has no chance of succeeding.

CHOOSING COACHES FOR EXECUTIVES: INTERNAL OR EXTERNAL

Whether to use internal or external coaches, especially for senior-level leaders and executives, isn't always easy to determine. There are advantages and disadvantages to each, depending on the situation. (Recall that an internal coach is employed by the organization to coach its employees, whereas an external coach works as an independent contractor or is employed by an outside coaching company.) What's most important is that executives be provided a coaching environment where they can open up and share honestly with the person who is coaching them.

To decide which to use, each organization will have to carefully evaluate the pros and cons of both options. Due diligence will help the organization gain clarity as to what is best for its leaders. Whichever choice is made, it's vital that the coaching environment be a safe one, offering credibility, confidentiality, and trust, in order to best serve the leaders being coached.

Choosing External Coaches

If greater objectivity is desired, external coaches may be best, for although they understand corporate culture generally, they won't have in-depth knowledge of the particular organization (though they will gain corporate knowledge over time if they work with several leaders in the same company). This can be a plus, as it enables them to assess the culture objectively, without filters or bias.

Organizations that have confidentiality concerns about hiring external coaches can ask them to sign nondisclosure statements, to ensure that proprietary information is protected. Interestingly, many senior leaders and executives actually prefer working with someone outside their own company because they feel confidentiality is easier to maintain.

CHOOSING INTERNAL COACHES

Internal coaches, of course, have the benefit of knowing the company from the inside but this may make it more difficult for them to be objective. However, if an in-depth understanding of the corporate culture is what's needed, it may be best to assign leaders to work with internal coaches, who know the climate, the political dynamics, and the culture.

More and more organizations are hiring or training internal people as coaches, to function either in specific business units or in HR or OD functions where they can serve as full-time coaches or as both HR/OD professionals and coaches. When they fill a dual role, internal coaches must be clear about which role they are playing, when. Again, confidentiality is critical if the coaching relationship is to be effective.

Taking Action

- How is your organization preparing for its future leadership needs?
- What is your organization doing proactively to prepare current and emerging leaders?
- What other options do you need to consider for getting enough people ready for leadership positions?

NOTES

1. To learn more about the Myers-Briggs Type Indicator survey, go to www.myersbriggs.org.
2. To learn more about the DiSC Profile, go to www.discprofile.com.
3. To learn more about EQ mapping, go to www.eq.org/EQ_Tools/ Assessment.

4. Scott Blanchard, Dr. Drea Zigarmi, and Dr. Vicky Essary, "The Leadership Profit Chain; Defining the Importance of Leadership Capacity," The Ken Blanchard Companies, 2005.

5. Jim Collins, *Good to Great: Why Some Companies Make the Leap and Others Don't* (New York: Harper Collins, 2001), 36.

CHAPTER 9

Team and Group Coaching

HAVE YOU EVER THOUGHT about the terms *team* and *group*? Each is an assemblage of people, yet important differences between the two exist. Complicating the issue is that each organization will have its own definitions for the terms. That said, a number of general distinctions can be made, as follows:

Teams:
- Share a common vision, purpose, and values.
- Are often long-term in nature, depending on their purpose.
- Pull together in the same direction, to achieve a common goal.
- Are composed of members who need each other to accomplish the common goal.

Athletic coaches offer an appropriate metaphor for the difference between coaching an individual versus coaching a team. A tennis coach will, for example, help a single player to sharpen his or her game. A basketball coach, in contrast, will focus on getting team members to work together, while leveraging the strengths of individuals, mitigating weaknesses, and creating partnerships and systems within the team. A coach for an individual will always put the best interest of that player ahead of anyone else; for the team coach, the best interests of the group will come first.

Groups:
- Come together for a specific purpose, such as to learn a new skill set, to support each other during a challenging time, or to give input on a specific topic.
- Can be short- or long-term arrangements.
- Are composed of members who do not necessarily need each other to achieve the common goal.

Two other terms that must be distinguished are *team coach* and *team leader*:

- The team leader may be a subject matter expert (SME), but may not have the skills to get the best from the individual members. Therefore, organizations will often provide a coach for a high-visibility, high-stakes team to ensure its success, because often even a good leader is too wrapped up in the day-to-day operations of the team to maintain objectivity.
- A team coach is not an expert in "team building," although he or she will be competent in managing group dynamics. Team building is usually required when a new team is being formed or is trying to recover from a failure or problem of some sort—especially when there is even one member sowing dissension and negativity. Teams that are coached from the outset usually don't need team building to restore motivation. Their mutual success motivates them! The more successful a team is, the more likely it is to stick together, manage stress, and surmount obstacles.

Certain coaching techniques can be applied successfully in both team and group settings. However, the requirements of the coach will vary depending on the exact nature of the assembly at hand.

TEAM COACHING

"Why do we need a coach?" asked Maria, the leader of a team tasked with getting a new software package to market. "I've got the right people, and we know what we're doing, Pete. We've had some problems, but nothing I can't handle."

"Your team is doing well, Maria, I agree," said Pete, Maria's boss, "but there are some red flags. You keep pushing back your milestones, and there seems to be some blaming and finger-pointing going on."

Pete continued: "Furthermore, your people are coming to me, asking me for feedback on their teammates—at least one of whom is either late every day or leaves early or both. I know you have the technical expertise, Maria, and you have good people, but right now you do need some help reestablishing trust and commitment. I cannot afford to have this project to backslide. Working with a coach will give you the support and focus you all can use to get back on track and stay on track. Think of it as an insurance policy."

In addition to all of the basic coach competencies (discussed in Chapter 4), a team coach understands the communication standards necessary for a group of people to work together to accomplish a common goal. In short, the team coach knows what is required to make the sum of the parts greater than the whole.

NOTE

Confidentiality is as critical to the success of team coaching as it is to individual coaching. No good can come when a team coach betrays confidences, takes sides, or, worse, "triangulates" between members. Certain individuals on the team will naturally try to influence the coach. When this happens, the coach must direct these individuals to others on the team or to the team as a whole, reminding them to use the agreed-on communication tools.

THE TEAM COACH'S TOOLBOX

Much research has been done to understand the characteristics of great teams. Whether a championship sports team or the team headed by Ernest Shackleton[1] in the 1914–1916 Antarctic expedition (not a single man died after they had to abandon their ship and were stranded on the ice for many months),[2] all highly successful teams share common goals, and it is the responsibility of the team coach to ensure these are discussed and agreed upon, up front. Even children who set out to build a tree house will draw up a set of rules that all must abide by. Unfortunately, in organizations, all too often, the need to do this is less obvious. Instead, assumptions are made about expectations and when not everyone shares the same assumptions, it results in discord and discontentment among team members.

Therefore, one of the first steps a team coach must take is to gain consensus as to how everyone will deal with every possible scenario the team will face. As part of this, values and behavioral standards for everyone on the team must be defined at the outset.

The team, at its inception, should discuss:

- Purpose and goal
- Vision and values
- Norms
- Roles

PURPOSE AND GOALS

Ultimately, a team is formed because doing so is the only way to accomplish a common goal. If the goal could be accomplished by one or two people, obviously, there would be no reason to form a team—especially given that the difficulty of getting things done increases with the addition of each new member to a team. Thus, whenever a team is formed, there has to be a clear purpose and an explicit goal.

Vision and Values

The team leader may have a clear vision of what he or she wants the team to accomplish, but it is rare that the vision is articulated in a clear and compelling way. When all members of the team work together to craft a *shared* vision, the chances are greater of achieving universal buy-in for that vision.

Values, too, must be set and shared. These can be developed with help from the coach, who can solicit from each team member his or her personal sense of what is most important when working with others. For example, the coach may learn that some team members value timeliness and accurate record-keeping. Others may value the idea that every voice be heard and everyone be treated equally. Ultimately, the team can use majority rule to prioritize what will be most important. Admittedly, going through the discussions about what is most important to arrive at shared values can be time-consuming and grueling; however, sharing values can help the team avoid all kinds of trouble down the line. Sadly, too often teams don't start talking about shared values until *after* trouble and/or emotional upheaval have occurred. You can think of developing shared values up front as similar to putting up hurricane window protectors before the wind starts blowing. A coach can help a team think through critical elements before a storm brews so that they are well prepared to work more effectively to weather the storm as a cohesive unit.

Norms

After the values have been prioritized, coaches can help a team clarify its code of conduct—which results in its "norms." The code of conduct should include clear consequences for failure to abide by the code. For example, if timeliness is an agreed-upon value, then an aspect of the code of conduct might be to schedule all meetings for 15 minutes past the hour so that everyone has time to get from previous meetings. The norm becomes that meetings will start on time, with all members in attendance and no excuses.

Finally, a well-functioning team will establish clear standards and agreements regarding communications—voice mail, email, and memos. This will result in the norms of a clear, common language and efficiency among team members.

ROLES

It is also key that teams identify who will play what role. Where people's job titles and levels of authority or specific areas of expertise are clearly defined, role determination is more clear-cut. But where there is confusion or overlap of responsibility, problems of ownership will inevitably arise. A coach can help untangle such problems by asking questions about possibly ill-informed assumptions. A good exercise to help with this is to have all team members write down what they believe their areas of responsibility to be, in order of importance, and then share them with their fellow team members. Most will be surprised by their expectations and assumptions, many of them faulty.

THE OPERATING MANUAL

Once the major decisions in the aforementioned areas have been made, the team should create an operating manual. Highly successful teams do this to avoid escalation of problems, as doing so is a well-proven problem-solving method. The operating manual, sometimes called a team charter or simply rules, should include, at a minimum, guidelines for how the team will make decisions and handle conflicts or problems. In addition a team may also develop guidelines that describe how to share new ideas, run meetings, and handle change.

A simple and useful tool for this purpose, used by the Blanchard Coaching team, is called Responsibility Charting.[3] For each task, goal, or deliverable the team decides:

- Who will be *responsible* for moving the ball forward and keeping others informed/involved
- Who needs to *approve* changes or decisions
- Who needs to be *consulted* for creative input and to provide relevant viewpoints and information
- Who will directly *participate* in subtasks
- Who needs to be kept *informed*

The key words used to create a chart (see Table 9.1) are:

Approves (A)
Responsible (R)
Consulted (C)
Participate (P)
Informed (I)

Using this model creates a common language and a simple discipline for comprehensive communication and inclusion, and

Table 9.1
Sample Responsibility Chart

Team Task or Goal	Kate (Team Leader)	Nick (HR Rep)	Susan (Team Member)	Tim (Team Member)	James (Team Member)
Recruit new hires	I	R, P	C	C	C
Interview new hires	I	R	C, P	C, P	C, P
Make final hiring decisions	R	A	P	P	I
Orient new hires	I	R	P	I	P
Integrate new hires into projects	P	C	R	C, I	C, I

helps avoid the kinds of power plays that can unwittingly sabotage another team member and/or the team at large. Note that the team coach must be vigilant about recording agreements on the responsibility chart. The coach also should redirect attention to the chart when disagreements arise so that appropriate discussions can take place and team members can move forward without lingering resentment or grudges.

Making It Real

- How clearly defined are roles in your organization?
- How can you customize the responsibility chart for your particular team?

The coach's role in all of this is to ensure that all team members are contributing to the development of the vision, values, and norms, and are clear about roles. The coach also makes sure that there is a time for discussion and that all team members, including the leader, abide by the agreements. That means the coach is responsible for pointing out when a team member steps over the agreed-upon bounds.

Ideally, as with any coaching engagement, once the initial setup has been facilitated, a team will be able to self-regulate and will only need an occasional correction by the coach.

Making It Real

- When you consider purpose and goals, vision and values, norms and roles, which do you think the teams in your organization need to give the most attention to?
- What steps will you take to guide the teams in this direction?

GROUP COACHING

Group coaching can be highly beneficial, marginally useful, or a dismal failure. A key to successful group coaching is to put into practice the lessons learned in the "school of hard knocks" by group coaches during the past 20 years, as described in this section.

WHY COACH GROUPS?

Group coaching can be tremendously useful for working with a small number of cohorts who have received some kind of long-term training that now requires a refresher or behavioral change. It can also be useful for individual contributors who are seeking extra support to accomplish a particularly challenging goal that requires a persistent effort over a short period of time. When done properly, group coaching can provide continued inspiration after a learning event, along with the structure, support, and accountability most people need to align their behavior to organizational norms in the absence of constant pressure to do so.

MODELS FOR GROUP COACHING

The group coaching process is extremely flexible and can be modeled to suit the specific needs of any group(s).

- Groups can meet in person or on the phone. To date, there is no evidence to suggest that meeting in person is more effective than meeting virtually. Many groups are composed of members who do not work in the same physical location, making telephone or videoconference meetings more time- and cost-efficient.
- Groups can meet on any schedule to fit the needs of the group—weekly, biweekly, daily, or monthly.

- Groups can be made up of individual contributors or cohorts from a specific class.
- Members can be assigned to a group or may self-select.

Many organizations have discovered group coaching to be an excellent way to promote development or sustain the application of learning, and it can be significantly less expensive than providing each individual with a personal coach.

NOTE

Coaches who are facilitating small groups must be experts in the specific training or at the specific development level the coaching is meant to promote.

SUCCESSFUL GROUP COACHING

Successful group coaching experiences share a number of characteristics, itemized in the following subsections.

Shared Purpose

Every group has to have a reason to exist, and a clear and compelling reason to meet regularly. These days, everyone faces overbooked calendars, making any activities that do not generate revenue or solve the myriad day-to-day problems not worthwhile. Each individual in the coaching group has to be given a compelling reason why he or she is being asked to show up to at these meetings.

Group coaching works well to support a group in using new behaviors or skills learned in a training program, and to provide support and inspiration to individuals who are developing new habits or working to achieve a goal.

Clearly Stated Individual Goals

These goals must include mileposts, for check-in at each meeting. One way to create a sense of urgency and interest in a coaching group is to assign each individual a goal that is broken down into segments, whose progress can be reported on at each meeting. Following these reports, individuals can either ask for help to brainstorm solutions to obstacles or to get recognition and celebrate success with the group.

Sense of Commitment

Making attendance at group coaching sessions mandatory may seem contrary to encouraging commitment to the process, but it actually goes a long way toward achieving just that, as it helps people realize the importance of the process and the importance of their participation in it. Attendance can be tracked and reported to management. Or each individual can be asked to write a personal commitment statement for delivery at the first group meeting. A third option is to pair members as "reporting teams" to encourage a shared commitment to the coaching initiative. Finally, penalties may be imposed for failure to attend group meetings.

Adequate Preparation

Group coaching sessions should be structured enough so that participants can feel progress in meeting their goals, yet loose enough to allow for natural emergence of valuable learning. To accomplish this balancing act, the coach needs to stay present in the moment and maintain a strong sense of where the group is headed. Less is more, in terms of structure.

Strong, Compelling Coach Presence

A group coach must be a strong leader, one who can command the group's respect and direct its focus. The coach's communication style should be clear, concise, and to the point. In fact, he or she should speak less than anyone else during the meeting, communicating mainly to greet individuals, direct/redirect attention, request clarity, and facilitate discussion. It is the members of the group who should be adding the most value. As one Blanchard group coach, Judith Wilson, put it: "The coach needs to listen for the question to be asked next."

The coach must pay close attention to each individual in the group, and track his or her comments. Many coaches keep a roster and make a checkmark next to each person's name when he or she participates. Then, if three-fourths of the way through the meeting, the coach has not heard from someone, he or she can solicit that person's input by saying, for example, "Joe, what do you think about that?" or "Leesa, what can you add to that?" Participants should know in advance that they will be called on if they are not actively participating. Conversely, the coach may need to "reel in" group members who are talking too much, becoming repetitive, or no longer adding value to the conversation. In sum, it is the responsibility of the coach to pay attention to the time arc of the meeting and make sure that everyone participates.

The coach should resist the urge to be the "expert," as doing so will dampen the desire of others to share their knowledge. The coach can "source the room,⁴ to discover group members who are sources of information, or experts, on particular topics. The coach can, of course, provide relevant information when necessary, or introduce topics or focus areas for each meeting. The coach can also solicit information or request that members of the group with specific expertise share small bits of information that might help members achieve goals.

Finite Timeline

A successful group coaching experience will have a defined beginning, middle, and end. All participants must be clear on the start date, must understand the dates and times of all meetings, and must be working toward the conclusion, when successes will be celebrated. The coaching group should be documenting and experiencing their journey together, so that it has significance to and meaning for each individual.

Connections throughout the Process

The coach needs to keep track of "aha" moments and discoveries, and make connections from one meeting to another. The coach also must be able to gauge when to focus on one person, who might benefit from an in-depth discussion on a certain topic, and when to turn what one group member says into a lesson for all. The coach should track accomplishments and changes, and point them out, as they occur over time.

Ground Rules for Communication

As with a team, in a group, all members should agree on norms at the beginning of their journey together. The coach can point out any break in norms and request ideas from the group about how to address the infraction.

Effective communication is key to establishing positive group dynamics. Best practices for a coach in this regard involve:

- Sending out a brief email after each meeting whose contents include: a list of the top three learning points generated at the meeting; a reminder of any homework that the group agreed to; and a reminder of the date, time, and location of the next meeting.
- Announcing via email, two to three days before the next meeting, the agenda of the upcoming meeting, along with a reminder to bring homework.
- Communicating intermittently between sessions, via email or voice mail, to offer small bits of information, or introduce concepts to inspire thought (no more than one per week). These messages could include quotes, relevant facts, or updates.

NOTE

These ideas work best in an email culture. For those organizations that are more voice-mail-oriented, messages will have to be very well-crafted and succinct.

Safe, Confidential Environment

The coach must never use sarcasm or tease a group member. Coaching rules apply at all times, to create a healthy, safe environment for exchange. In addition, members must agree at the outset to maintain the confidentiality of the group, and commit to never discussing outside the group what goes on within the group, unless explicit permission has been granted to do so, in special circumstances.

Making It Real

- How would you prioritize the keys to successful group coaching for your organization?
- Are there other keys that you would add to the list?
- How can you help groups in your organization function more effectively?

CONCLUSION

Teams and groups are part of the fabric of corporate cultures. Individuals come together all the time to accomplish goals; make decisions; learn new skills; and produce better systems, processes, and products. Smart, effective leaders know when teams need coaching to help them be more efficient, to make the best use of everyone's time, and to leverage new ideas and knowledge. Effective group and team coaches have the skills and experience to facilitate meetings and help people move forward together.

Taking Action

- What are specific ways you can envision using team or group coaching in your organization?
- How might you initiate a discussion about using team or group coaching where you work?

NOTES

1. Alfred Lansing, *Endurance: Shackleton's Incredible Voyage* (New York: Carroll & Graf, 1999).
2. Margot Morrell, Stephanie Capparell, and Alexandra Shackleton, *Shackleton's Way: Leadership Lessons from the Great Antarctic Explorer* (New York: Penguin, 2002).
3. Richard Beckhard and Wendy Pritchard, *Changing the Essence: The Art of Creating and Leading Fundamental Change in Organizations* (San Francisco: Jossey-Bass, 1992), 83–84.
4. Term provided by Blanchard Coach Judith Wilson. Laura Goodrich also contributed to this section.

CHAPTER 10

Developing Master Coaching Skills

WHAT IS THE DIFFERENCE between a good coach and an excellent coach? What skills does a coach have that other professionals don't? How do coaches differentiate themselves from other helping and consulting professionals? The short answer is that coaches must have a lot going for them to be successful. In contrast to consultants who typically are experts in one or more subjects, coaches must master a much more difficult task: understanding how human beings accomplish tasks and goals. Likewise they must have a broad knowledge of how organizations function, with a solid grounding in business fundamentals, management basics, and leadership theory. Most coaches read voraciously to keep themselves informed in all these areas.

Organizations implementing coaching initiatives today recognize that coaching comprises specific competencies, hence now prefer the coaches they work with to be certified by the International Coach Federation (ICF).[1] Notably, since 2005, requests for ICF-certified coaches have tripled. (ICF certification is based on a person's coach-specific training; they must also be able to offer proof of a certain number of hours spent coaching and to demonstrate competence in specific areas).

CRUCIAL COACHING COMPETENCIES

Our years of experience in recruiting and deploying coaches to organizations of all kinds have revealed a number of crucial competencies professionals in this field need to have to be effective in their work. The following sections define and describe these coaching competencies, which are divided into four distinct categories:

- General coaching competencies
- Corporate coaching competencies
- Executive coaching competencies
- Master coaching competencies

GENERAL COACHING COMPETENCIES

These are the basics. All coaches should have a solid grounding in these competencies.

Service Orientation

Picture a tugboat, purely a service vessel. Though humble and small, the tugboat has a powerful engine, capable of guiding ships much bigger than itself in or out of a harbor. But it takes more than the power of the tugboat to make this happen. The captains of both the tugboat and the large ship have to agree on their mutual goals and how they will accomplish them. Clearly, a tugboat can't force a big ship to do something it has not agreed to do.

Coaches, too—especially novices—must be aware at all times of the reciprocal nature of the relationships they form with their clients. It is not enough to want to be of service; clients must want to, agree to, be coached.

It's also important for coaches to maintain a healthy perspective on their work, and to find ways to get their personal needs met outside their lives. By doing so, they will be better able to focus on and serve their clients.

Self-Knowledge

For coaches to be effective to others, they must first be extremely well-informed about their own values, needs, interests, abilities, personality type, sensitivities, hot buttons, and so forth. In short, coaches should be keenly aware of anything and everything about themselves that might affect how they come across to other people.

Ability to Be Present

The ability to be completely present in the moment is one of the most difficult competencies for coaches—as it is for us all. Coaches must be able to put aside their personal worries and to-do lists, and quiet their self-critical voices and all of the other "noise" that keep them from paying full attention to what's happening with their clients. People being coached will know when the coach is distracted, and won't feel they are being well served.

Ability to Connect

Needless to say, not every person being coached will be able to relate well with the coach to whom they've been assigned. However, the reverse *should* be true. Highly skilled coaches need to be able to connect with those they coach, pure and simple.

The ability to connect can be broken down into several sub-competencies, for greater comprehension:

- Deep respect for and willingness to value all people, regardless of their foibles and flaws
- Adaptability to different thinking/learning styles and cultural norms
- Ability to put aside personal preferences, especially when they differ from those of the person being coached
- Knowledge of one's own personality traits and their potential impact on other personality types

Ability to Build Trust and Respect

Building trust and respect is integrally related to the previous competency, ability to connect. Trust is built out of the sum total of all the competencies. Respect is earned through a consistent display of competence, especially at senior levels.

Each person being coached will, of course, accord trust and respect based on his or her own set of personal values, but there are a number of factors that go a long way toward ensuring coaches will be trusted and respected by their clients. Coaches must exhibit:

- Consummate professionalism (described later in the chapter)
- Subject matter knowledge
- Organization and industry awareness
- Ironclad confidentiality. (Remember, as described repeatedly in this book, coaches who discuss inappropriately the individuals they are coaching are breaking the implicit code of ethics and/or written agreements.)

Ability to Match Personal Style with Client Style

Whether a coach and client are matched by someone in the organization, or the coach is selected personally by the individual, it is the coach's responsibility to take note of and match as closely as possible that person's style preferences. And at advanced levels, a coach may be called on not only to match the client's style but also to influence the style of the person being coached, should the need arise.

Style issues include:

- *Energy.* Is the person a low-energy type? Is he or she anxious? Does he or she speak too loudly, or quietly? The coach must notice all this and bring to the person's attention any behavior that needs adjustment.
- *Thinking style and speed.* If a coach responds to an analytical thinker with a conceptual response, it will interrupt

the process flow. Likewise, if the coach slows down a lightning-speed thinker with poorly timed questions, or vice versa. Note: Novice coaches should curb a natural tendency to make judgments about thinking style and speed, and to try to influence it, before they have earned trust and respect.

- *Humor*. The use of humor in the coaching environment needs to be handled carefully. Those who normally use humor to navigate their world must curb the tendency to overdo it until they understand how it will be taken by the person being coached. Humor is deeply tied to culture, personal history, language habits, and religious and/or spiritual background. What one person thinks is funny another might find offensive, so it's vital to tread lightly, so as not to damage the coaching relationship unintentionally. Coaches must be patient and wait for cues from their clients. The same goes with irreverence. And, note, the use of obscenity and profanity is almost never appropriate!

Ability to Listen

We discussed at length in an earlier chapter the importance of the ability to listen, but it bears repeating here. Simply, coaches who are not good listeners do not stay employed as coaches for very long.

Here are some additional guidelines for this critical competency:

1. At the most fundamental level, a coach should: hear what is being said, reflect back to check for accuracy, and show evidence of understanding what was said. As coaches listen, they also should pay attention to style, personality type, communication preferences, and sense of humor of the person being coached.

2. At the next level, the coach should be listening, for values, needs, and any other information that has bearing on the conversation. The coach also should be able to discern what is *not* being said and to draw it out. In drawing out underlying information, the coach can better serve the person being coached.

3. Master listeners not only hear what is not being said, they also can also pick up on what the person being coached might not be aware he or she is really feeling. For example, when Sue was continually late for meetings, her HR professional, Tamara, called her in for a meeting. As they started to talk, Tamara realized that Sue seemed unhappy in her job even though Sue had said nothing to indicate that was the case. So Tamara casually remarked, "Sue, it seems like something has changed in your motivation and commitment to your job. What's really going on?"

Ability to Inquire

Closely linked to the ability to listen, an effective coach asks high-quality questions based on what he or she has heard and observed. In addition to crafting appropriate and helpful questions, the coach should constantly assess whether a given line of inquiry is the most useful one at the time, for the person being coached.

Novice coaches should guard against asking "filler questions," which really are tantamount to making small talk and have no real value. Yes, they take time for the person being coached to answer, and may even satisfy the need of the person being coached to talk about him- or herself, or satisfy the coach's curiosity, but that is not the purpose of the coaching process.

Filler questions to avoid include:

- Why did you do that?
- Then what happened?

- What did you do?
- Who is [the person being talked about]?
- Where is that?

Filler questions will often make the person being coached feel that they are wasting their time (which is the case), and do not contribute to the coaching conversation. Certainly, they do not move the person being coached forward in any meaningful direction.

As with listening, there are levels of inquiry:

1. *Clarifying questions.* The hallmark of active listening, clarifying questions ensure understanding about what is being communicated and helps to fill in knowledge gaps. Clarifying questions help the person being coached gain greater understanding. Just beware: Many clarifying questions are premature and unnecessary. Novice coaches, in particular, may tend to interrupt with their questions, instead of waiting for a more appropriate time. Clarifying questions for the benefit of the person being coached include:
   - What is the core of what you're saying?
   - What do you really think?
   - What does that mean?

   Clarifying questions for the benefit of the coach include:
   - Can I make sure I got this right?
   - Is there anything else you think I should know?
   - Could you give me a little more detail about this so I understand it better?
2. *Focus questions.* Focus questions set the direction for the dialogue that gives the person being coached the most leverage. Focus questions include:
   - Of all the things we could delve into right now, which is going to be most helpful to you?

- You've mentioned three different things. Where would you like to start?
- How can I help you with this right now?
- What do you want from this conversation?

3. *Discovery questions.* These questions generate new thinking, creative ideas, and breakthroughs in perspective for the person being coached. Discovery questions include:
   - If you could wave a magic wand and have this situation go exactly the way you want it to, what would occur?
   - If you were a risk taker, what would you do?
   - How do you think this will look to you a year from now?
   - If you were to do this perfectly, what would need to happen?
   - What is the most important point here?

4. *Challenging questions.* These questions test the assumptions and resolve of the person being coached. Challenging questions stimulate difficult introspection that can yield new insight for the person being coached. The right challenging question can even help the person being coached solidify a commitment to action. Challenging questions include:
   - What if you *could* do it? How would you start?
   - What is the worst thing that could happen?
   - How else might you look at this?
   - What do you *really* want?
   - What will cause the breakthrough here?
   - What would happen if you raised your standards?

Capacity to Offer and Accept Feedback

Sometimes a coach is given feedback from others in the organization that he or she is expected to share with the person being coached. Or the coach may have personal observations he or she wants to bring to the attention of the person being coached. In a coaching relationship where trust and respect have been established, feedback is often welcome; but in offering feedback, coaches must restrain the desire to tell people what to do and try to change them. Feedback also must be timely and connected to something important to the person being coached (*not* to the coach). Feedback that is not relevant to the person being coached is just noise.

One effective way for coaches to approach feedback is to ask permission to share the information. If the person agrees, then the coach should share the feedback in a way appropriate to the person being coached. If the person declines, the coach should respect that decision—though the choice not to hear the feedback might subsequently become a topic for coaching.

Conversely, coaches must be able to solicit feedback about themselves and about the quality of their coaching, and then be willing to make appropriate changes, to demonstrate flexibility and adaptability. In this way, coaches serve as role models, demonstrating how to respond graciously to feedback with gratitude and thoughtfulness.

Ability to Rein In Desire to Give Advice

Many coaches get into the field because they are gifted at giving advice and helping people figure out what to do. Unfortunately, giving advice is not coaching, and indulging the desire to do so can be detrimental to a coaching relationship. True, coaches are often asked to brainstorm ideas and to share information, but doing so can be tricky and so must be approached with caution. The key factor is the coach's ability to be sensitive to the receptivity of the person being coached. The coach must also be able to manage his or her need to be right, to be useful, to be admired.

NOTE

This competency is often overlooked and misunderstood, especially by those who have been extremely successful in roles requiring a problem-solving ability.

Willingness to Challenge

Knowing when and how to challenge is essential to effective coaching. Challenging a person being coached can only be done successfully if the coach has first established trust and respect.

Several factors are involved in the ability to challenge appropriately:

- *Timing*: There are those who can be challenged in the first 10 minutes of the first coaching conversation. In fact, some clients won't respect a coach who isn't willing to throw down the gauntlet at the outset! Others need time to develop a strong working relationship before they can accept a challenge. Coaches must evaluate the style of the person being coached and time their challenges appropriately.
- *Permission*: The coach must ask permission to challenge the person being coached. Gaining permission to challenge is not optional, but methods vary according to the style of the person being coached. For example, a coach might ask, "May I have permission to challenge you on the belief that's behind the statement you just made?"
- *Content*: The rule of thumb is to ask a little more of the person being coached than he or she thinks is achievable. A fine line exists between choosing a challenge that will inspire awe and hope—as in, "Wow, could I really do that?"—and the one that will provoke disbelief, as in, "Oh, that will never happen."
- *Language*: Knowing how to ask for something is as important as knowing what to ask for. This requires a coach's attention to context, history, and use of language. For example, some people respond well to sports metaphors; others prefer quotes from poets. People without children will probably not respond to parenting parallels. Although this may seem obvious, it is surprising how many coaches use metaphors or examples that do not resonate with the person being coached.
- *Risk-taking*: The coach should take occasional risks. Challenging a person being coached can sometimes backfire, and the coach should be ready to deal with that possibility.

Ability to Share Multiple Perspectives

Good coaches are adept at seeing both the forest and the trees. Often, it makes sense to use inquiry to help the person being coached acknowledge alternative, useful perspectives, so the coach should offer other ways to look at something. Note, however, that a coach who is gifted at systems thinking, or is highly creative, will have to rein in the need to share everything he or she sees as a possibility, for doing so only serves the coach's ego, not the need of the person being coached. The key is to share other perspectives only when they are most useful.

Ability to Remain Neutral

Coaches have to be hypervigilant not to reveal or impose their personal beliefs and agendas regarding "hot topics" such as gender, race, politics, and religion. The more obvious ones will, of course, be the easiest to avoid; it's those that coaches may be unaware of that can rear their heads unexpectedly. For example, coaches who are corporate "refugees" may be driven to "save" midlevel managers from what the coaches regard as an unfulfilling career choice. Or, coaches with a strong feminist agenda may inadvertently encourage a person being coached to take actions that are not necessarily aligned with that individual's values.

In certain circumstances, coaches may even choose to inform a person being coached about issues they have difficulty treating objectively. After all, coaches are human, and naming and claiming their own problem areas can be used to increase trust.

Mental Agility

Coaches working at senior levels in organizations come in contact with intelligent and accomplished people, who talk fast, think fast, switch subjects frequently and at high speed, and in general are overachievers. Novice coaches may mistakenly "misdiagnose" such highly intelligent and creative people as having attention deficit disorder. This is never helpful! People being coached need their coaches to keep up with them, and will become annoyed if they are forced to slow down.

Needless to say, coaches will not be able to work with everyone effectively, but as a matter of course, coaches should come prepared to alter their own preferred thinking style and learn how to be comfortable, no matter whom they are working with. Having the ability to shift thinking modes is an extremely important aspect of mental agility. It helps the coach do excellent work with a broad range of people. The key is for coaches to be agile enough and aware of the preferred thinking styles of their clients so as to be able to honor their needs. This does not mean that it is never appropriate to introduce another perspective, as mentioned previously; but the coach should remember to ask permission to guide the person being coached in a potentially useful alternative thought process. Usually, the person being coached will agree, and appreciate being taught a new thinking style. Permission is the critical factor.

Skilled at Different Thinking Styles

Coaches need to be able to adjust their thinking style to the person and the situation at hand.

- *Strategic thinking.* A coach should be able to take a broad-scale, long-term view of the person being coached and his or her situation, helping to assess options and the implication of choices. One of the greatest services a coach can provide is to help the person being coached thoughtfully define his or her best result. The coach can take a "mental helicopter ride," to view the big picture, in order to help the person being coached see other perspectives and make new discoveries that will enhance his or her decision-making process.
- *Conceptual thinking.* Often, analytical thinking is lumped in with conceptual thinking, but it deserves separate mention in the context of coaching, for two reasons. One, the coach

collects data points over time and often needs to synthesize seemingly unrelated data streams to cobble together a new idea or perspective, and this requires conceptual thinking. Synthesizing in this way comes from the ability to keep in mind many concepts over time in order to generate something related but altogether fresh. Two, occasionally a person being coached may patch together ideas and make big conceptual leaps without "connecting the dots." An effective coach who is a conceptual thinker can help the person being coached reach the goal most efficiently.

- *Systems thinking.* Coaches who are skilled at systems thinking are able to observe the environment and the structures in it, and determine how it all either contributes or fails to contribute to the success of the person being coached. The coach should be able to help clients to acknowledge systems and understand how they fit into them—that is, engage in rather than stand apart from them.

  There are many useful tools to help people being coached see the bigger picture, or to work through the complexity of a situation. Depending on how visual the person being coached is, diagramming a concept on a whiteboard may be helpful. An experienced coach can identify patterns and point them out to people being coached. This particular competency is useful for coaches working with people who either don't think in terms of systems or who think *only* this way.

- *Analytical thinking.* Analytical thinking is often defined as critical thinking or critical reasoning. Coaches who excel at this type of thinking process should guard against relying too heavily on the skill. However, when working with people who are of the same type, and can reason an argument all the way through, the coach should be able to follow the thought processes. In organizational work, a coach should be able to analyze complex situations, breaking each into its constituent parts, then be able to recognize and assess several likely causal factors and ways of interpreting the information.

A coach also should be able to identify connections that are not obvious. (This relates to the ability to synthesize, discussed earlier.) When working with senior leaders, coaches should be able to integrate information from diverse sources, often involving large amounts of information. Finally, it is helpful when a coach can think several steps ahead of his or her clients, encouraging ideas for courses of action and anticipating likely outcomes.

Ability to Brainstorm Creatively

Brainstorming is helping the person being coached generate ideas; the more creative, the better. In the right circumstances, a real brainstorming session can be extremely useful. The coach should know the rules for brainstorming to facilitate it. Novice coaches, however, should be careful not to indulge in brainstorming more often than is strictly necessary. Often a simple review of the options will do.

Brainstorming guidelines are as follows:

- State the problem clearly.
- Allow no criticism, evaluation, judgment, or defense of ideas during the brainstorming session.
- Place no limits on ideas, no matter how outrageous or impractical they may seem. Every idea is to be expressed.
- Encourage quantity over quality.
- Encourage "piggybacking," or building on ideas.
- Record all ideas.

Although, traditionally, brainstorming involves more than two people, in the coaching relationship, two are usually enough. The key is to be sure that the person being coached starts the brainstorming session. This activity is an appropriate option when the person being coached seems stuck or limited in options. The coach might suggest that they brainstorm, and then ask the person being coached to start. Often, once the person being coached gets going, he or she will generate a number of options. If more good ideas are needed, the person being coached may want to gather a group of colleagues to help with the process. Just be sure the brainstorming rules apply with the group.

Ability to Remember

The ability to note and loop back to relevant threads in prior discussions is a critical skill for a coach. People being coached are often amazed when the coach recalls a remark made months earlier. A good memory is another way of building trust, as it demonstrates the coach has been paying attention. It also helps the person being coached to weave a strong fabric of self-discovery.

Ability to Empathize

A person being coached needs to know that the coach understands the situation and has had personal experience with frustration, fear, and unhappiness. The coach should be able to express understanding and care and, at the same time, be able to keep the person being coached moving—not let the person wallow. In rare cases, the coach may share personal information about a similar situation he or she has experienced. When this is the case, the coach should first ask permission, and if given, be brief so the conversation doesn't become about the coach. Personal sharing should be used judiciously. A reliable general rule is the more the coach is talking, the less effective they are being, so when sharing stories or information, get to the point.

Willingness to Serve as Advocate and Champion

The coach should be willing to support the person being coached, no matter what develops in the coaching process. A person being coached will know intuitively if the coach isn't being 100 percent supportive. In some cases, the coach may have to make a leap of faith about a person's ability to accomplish a goal in order to help the person being coached to do the same. It will take experience for a coach to gain the confidence to do this, but it is well worth the effort, as it is a powerful thing to do for a person being coached. If, however, a coach doesn't believe that the person being coached can accomplish a goal, the coach may recommend a change in the goal, a change in the coach, or reconsideration of the coaching effort itself.

The point is, the coach should serve as advocate and champion for the person being coached—to do whatever is in the best interest of that individual. In some cases, a coach will need to take a stand on behalf of what is personally important to the person being coached. This is distinct from the coach advocating for his or her own idea or agenda; it is supporting the idea or agenda of the person being coached.

Commitment to Maintain Professional Standards

A coach must set and maintain the highest standards of professionalism. He or she must:

- Be on time.
- Send only appropriate, well-written communications.
- Keep commitments.
- Use correct language.

These days, a critical factor in being able to maintain professional standards is the need to stay up to date technologically. The coach should have at least the same level of knowledge and technological capability as his or her clients—although, ideally, the coach will be a little more advanced. Coaches need to be able to help their clients learn how to leverage technology in the workplace, from the appropriate use of email to how to stay connected when out of the office. No coach should ever have to tell a client, for example, that he or she cannot download a document because he is on dial-up—which, by the way, is a true story.

Willingness to Go Above and Beyond

The attentive coach goes above and beyond the defined coaching requirements to create added value for the person being coached, as another way to encourage and motivate the client. For example, a coach might send a relevant book to a client who likes to read, or, conversely, a synopsis of that book to one who doesn't. A coach might make a phone call between sessions to offer support to a client who is facing an important presentation to the board—or send an email with an inspirational quotation, or another form of encouragement. When reading the paper, a coach might think, "Joe would find this interesting. I'll scan it and email it to him." Or, when listening to the radio, a coach may recognize that Mary would be interested in hearing about the new association being started for businesswomen in her area.

Though coaches are being paid to create an environment in which people will grow, and clients are of course aware of that, it's the mark of a good coach to want to do just a little more, on his or her own time, to solidify a coaching relationship.

Ability to Set and Maintain Boundaries

There is always the risk that coaches might become too friendly with their clients; certainly, close friendships have grown from coaching relationships. But this is appropriate only after the coaching relationship has been officially terminated. While the coaching is in progress, appropriate professional boundaries must be set and observed. This can be tricky, however, because professional boundaries are established on a case-by-case basis. That said, generally, it is recommended that a coach:

- Refrain from socializing with clients during the coaching process.
- Communicate with clients using only business contact numbers.

- Avoid communicating outside of business hours, unless it is to leave a message, and is absolutely necessary.
- Never discuss personal issues in any detail, unless an experience has critical relevance to the client's situation.

Knowledge and Understanding of Client's Business

Having some degree of knowledge and understanding of the client's field of work is essential to the coaching initiative. For example, a salesperson will need a coach who understands the selling process, who has a strong grounding in sales process models, and has compassion for the difficulties inherent to the sales profession.

Industry experience is a plus, though not absolutely crucial for a coach to be successful. However, coaches who don't have experience in their clients' fields should be able to climb the learning curve quickly, to understand the inner workings of their business—for example, how it generates revenue and tracks profitability, how people are compensated and rewarded, what the "lingo" is, and so forth. The coach also should learn how the client training base works, how the performance review system is set up, and what models and systems are in use in the business.

Understanding of Human Development

For coaches to be truly effective, they will need a basic understanding of life-stage development. A great deal of information is available on this topic. One source we recommend is Frederic M. Hudson's *The Adult Years: Managing the Art of Self-Renewal* (San Francisco: Jossey-Bass Inc., 1999). With this knowledge, coaches will be better prepared to offer useful perspectives and alternative ways of thinking in regard to the various stages of development in individuals of all ages.

Many coaches work best with individuals who are either one or two steps ahead or one step behind them developmentally. Experience suggests coaches closer to their clients developmentally are able to stay more interested, and "fresh." The coaching relationship is a dynamic, creative partnership, so both parties need to be actively and equally engaged.

Making It Real

- Of the general coaching competencies listed, which do you think would be the most crucial in your organization right now?
- What steps can you take to ensure that any potential coaches for your organization are competent in those areas?

CORPORATE COMPETENCIES

Coaches working in organizations will need these competencies.

Organizational Savvy

A coach working in an organization must have a strong understanding of how companies are set up, including the different ways in which organization charts are built and the history behind the structure.

Business Acumen

For credibility purposes, a coach should understand business basics, that is, have a broad range of knowledge about how businesses run, including:

- Distinction between revenue and profits
- Basic business functions
- How strategic planning is done
- How HR rules and process are set
- Criteria used to set policies and procedures in different functional areas
- Basic understanding of project management

Understanding of Management Basics

A coach should have a solid grounding in the basics of management skill sets. Often, individuals being coached will need a little just-in-time tune-up in basics, similar to the regular one-to-one weekly or biweekly meetings between the manager and the employee, when they catch up, address questions, review tasks and responsibilities, brainstorm, and solve problems. These basics include goal setting, performance planning, timely feedback, and appropriate direction and support.

Political Awareness

An effective organizational coach has a healthy grasp of the power dynamics common to all organizations, and is willing and able to share this insight with people being coached. The coach understands that power is not always related to position, and so can help the person being coached to work on his or her personal power base and leverage that to achieve goals.

Cross-Cultural Insight

With the global economy, coaches today often are called upon to work with individuals from all over the world, from cultures very different from their own. Coaches should therefore become familiar with the cultural implications of those they are working with. Having this awareness and sensitivity will help them to gain greater professional credibility, enabling them to help the person being coached understand when cultural differences might impact success.

A number of excellent resources are available to help coaches and others understand the business implications of cross-cultural issues. Two books we recommend are: *Managing Across Cultures* (second edition), edited by Susan C. Schneider and Jean-Louis Barsoux (Prentice Hall, 2002), and *Coaching Across Cultures: New Tools for Leveraging National, Corporate, and Professional Differences* by Philippe Rosinski (London: Nicholas Brealey Publishing,

2003). And an outstanding Web site for coaches working across cultures or for clients who want to become more attuned to cultural issues is www.geert-hofstede.com.

Making It Real

- Of the several corporate coaching competencies listed, which do you think would be the most crucial in your organization right now?
- What steps can you take to ensure that any potential coaches for your organization are competent in those areas?

EXECUTIVE COMPETENCIES

Coaches who work at high levels of management in organizations should demonstrate a working knowledge of these competencies.

Understanding of Leadership Models in Play

There are multiple schools of thought on what makes a good business leader, and no shortage of research and information on the topic. Few, however, would argue that all great leaders have some fundamental things in common. They know how to:

- Articulate a vision and a direction for their company.
- Access the best possible minds to set a winning strategy.
- Hire the best available talent; they are comfortable surrounding themselves with people more knowledgeable than themselves.
- Communicate and serve as a role model for company values, in a compelling way.

Because there are so many models for great leadership, coaches need to be able to assess which are being used in the organization they are working in, to be able to help their individual clients. That is the only way they will be able to determine which metaphors and examples will be most compelling to the individuals they are coaching. An effective coach will thus be able to devise the most efficient and appropriate method for helping the person being coached build his or her own leadership model.

Recognition of Organizational Vision, Mission, Purpose

Organizational leaders are expected to formulate a clear picture of their companies' futures, including what they and their employees have to do to realize that vision. An executive coach can help business leaders use appropriate language to describe their companies' vision, mission, and purpose, so that they can communicate it companywide.

Executive Presence

People receiving coaching expect their coaches to present themselves professionally at all times. The coach must demonstrate maturity, experience, intelligence, self-confidence, and capability.

Executive coaches, in particular, must think carefully about the impression they are making at all times. This can be a challenge because focusing on externals can distract from the business at hand—the coaching process. Nevertheless, exhibiting an executive presence is, simply, a strategic part of the coaching process.

Such a presence is hard to describe, however, as it is the sum of many details:

- Physical strength, balance, and grace
- Intellectual confidence (not arrogance)
- Sense of being comfortable in one's skin
- Ability to stay present
- Ability to quiet the mind and tune out external distractions
- Attention to detail in personal presentation, including dress—well-kept shoes/briefcases/outerwear, well-cut and

maintained suits, professional hair care, and understated makeup for women

- Use of appropriate language and humor

Making It Real

- Of the several executive coaching competencies listed, which do you think would be the most crucial in your organization right now?
- What steps can you take to ensure that any potential coaches for your organization are competent in those areas?

MASTER COACH COMPETENCIES

Master coaches must have such a solid grounding in all coaching competencies at every level, enabling them to "coach the coaches." They will understand, and be able to explain, what to consider when a leader or manager uses a coach approach. They can readily identify, for example, when a coach is doing something that may prevent him or her from achieving the best results with their clients.

Master coaches will, of course, be able to identify the potential pitfalls inherent to coaches working in an organization. They have experience facing the challenges of any coaching culture, in organizations of various types, each of which has positives and negatives. To help other coaches develop their skills and competencies, master coaches will:

- Be attuned to the tendency that coaches, especially novices, sometimes have to frame everything as positive. This can confuse as well as annoy a person being coached.
- Caution those coaches who try to control, rather than guide, their clients. As noted throughout this book, successful coaching relationships are built on trust and mutual understanding, not control.

- Alert coaches against using specialized language or jargon, and risk leaving a person being coached mystified.
- Help coaches guard against the desire to integrate themselves into manager/employee relationships, instead of adding value as an objective professional. In a very real sense, coaches should be working to put themselves out of a job, not attempting to make themselves indispensable. Coaches must be very wary of making their clients dependent on them, on their opinions and guidance. The goal is always to help the person help him- or herself. It is crucial that coaches do not get carried away by their own importance.
- Guide managers who know just enough about coaching to be dangerous. Strong and attentive mentoring is in order to help these managers grow and be successful.

Master coaches have experience with all of these situations; they can teach others how to avoid them and how to deal with them if they do occur, despite best efforts.

ASSESSING COACH COMPETENCE

As you can see, the list of coach competencies is long, and so may seem daunting. How is it possible, then, given all these requirements, to determine whether a coach is competent? There is only one foolproof way: to watch that person in action, coaching. How is this possible? One way is to view a live or recorded coaching session—with permission, of course.

Or the coach can be asked to role-play a coaching session. In this case, there are a number of activities to be used to help assess coach competence. These are itemized in Table 10.1. Note that the format shown in the table assumes that:

- The interview is conducted over the phone.
- An hour has been set aside by both interviewer and coach.
- Coach has been identified as meeting initial criteria.
- Coach understands that this is a role-play.
- Coach is willing to receive development feedback.

Table 10.1

Assessing Coach Competence

Timing	Interviewer Activity
Introduction: 3–15 minutes	Welcome the coach. Check time assumptions. Explain structure of call. Tell the coach to assume a 20-minute coaching session and to take responsibility for structuring the time. Ask permission to give feedback at the end. Check for agreement. Check for questions, concerns.
Set up rules of engagement: 3–4 minutes	*Give an overview of what the coach would already know*: Describe the company, your role in it, level of responsibility, and your personality. *Set the context*: Explain this is the second call in a series of 10 coaching sessions. Explain what the coach knows and what has been accomplished; assume that respect and trust have been established. *Explain the situation*: Try to include at least three focus areas, such as career path, time management, communication, community, and self-concept. Do not identify the exact areas, just sketch the situations to make them fairly obvious and easy to diagnose. Give enough information to enable the coach to identify the focus areas, and then gradually hone in on one to work on. Check that the coach remembers to return to other issues in the course of the conversation. Watch for coach's tendency to focus too much on irrelevant areas. Explain that once the session starts you can both step in and out of the coaching by using a clear verbal signal: "Curtain up/down" works well, as does "game on/off" or "time out." Explain that you will stop the session to offer direction; and make sure the coach knows that he or she can stop the action at any time to get his or her bearings or to ask for process clarity.

(Continued)

Table 10.1

Assessing Coach Competence (*Continued*)

Timing	Interviewer Activity
Present problem: 3–7 minutes	*Begin the session.* Coach talent can be assessed by offering the following challenges: • Directing a person being coached who is all unfocused. • Drawing out and guiding a low-key or shy person. • Engaging a person being coached who doesn't think there is anything to work on.
Coach fully engages: 7–10 minutes	Interviewer should look for coach to: • Connect genuinely. • Focus intelligently and ask clarifying questions. A lot of why questions are the sign of a novice. Judging and accuracy assessment questions are egregious. • Match energy and style. • Be judicious in making suggestions and offering solutions.
Coach challenges person being coached: intermittent	Interviewer should look for coach to: • Share one or two principles, then ask the person being coached what has worked in the past and what might work now. • Ask the person being coached to step up to the plate if necessary. • Make a challenging request. • Stay calm, focused, and check in with interviewer. Interviewer should pay attention to how much they feel endorsed, heard, understood, or encouraged.
Assess viability of options: 3–5 minutes	Interviewer should look for coach to: • Continue brainstorming with person being coached and start to hone in on possible actions. • Ask how he or she can support the person being coached.

Table 10.1

Assessing Coach Competence (*Continued*)

Timing	Interviewer Activity
Check for impact: 1–2 minutes	Interviewer should assess the extent to which he or she feels confident about what will be done. Is the interviewer leaving the session with greater clarity than before? Did he or she discover something new during this call?
Wrap-up call: 3 minutes	Interviewer should look for coach to: • Keep an eye on the clock and wrap up the coaching session on time. (Note: If the coach loses track of time, and many do in an interview situation, give the coach about 3 more minutes to wrap up the call.) Interviewer should assess coach's ability to do this efficiently. • Ask: "What value did the person being coached get? Was the person being coached clear about prescribed actions? Was there anything the person being coached wishes the coach had done but didn't?"
End role-play/give feedback: 5 minutes	Interviewer should: • Call time. • Ask whether coach wants feedback. • Ask coach for his or her own assessment of call, including what went well and what did not. How a coach rates the coaching call is extremely revealing. Also, how the coach responds to interviewer feedback is equally revealing. Give feedback based on the following criteria from the perspective of the person being coached: • Did I feel heard and understood? • Was I ever interrupted or cut off? • Did I ever get shut down or was I ever made wrong?

(*Continued*)

Table 10.1

Assessing Coach Competence (*Continued*)

Timing	Interviewer Activity
	• Did I clarify my situation for myself?
	• Did I get any new insights?
	• Do I feel more confident about how I might proceed?
	• Did I learn anything that I can connect to the bigger picture of my life, or a principle that I will be able to apply usefully in the future?
	• Did the coach make me more important than his or her need to impress me and add value?
	• Am I crystal clear about an action that I agreed to take between now and our next conversation?
	To take feedback successfully, the coach's ability to listen well is vital. Defensiveness is unacceptable in a coach in this situation; the coach must demonstrate confidence, flexibility, grace, and maturity.
Wrap up interview	Interviewer should: • Make sure there are no lingering questions. • Ascertain and agree to timeline for next steps.
Do administrative follow-up	Interviewer should: • Pass on notes to relevant parties. • File interview notes for future reference.

IN CONCLUSION

Coaches have an amazing amount of wisdom and experience to share; they are trained to be good listeners and to have empathy for others and they have a genuine desire to be of service to others. Exceptional coaches have strong and well-considered opinions about how things should be done, and set high standards for themselves and those they work with. Coaches are excellent communicators and help their clients to be the same.

The wisest coaches also have given a great deal of thought to how they can achieve a balanced life for themselves, one that allows for self-care and makes time for the renewal necessary to remain in service to others. This enables them to help their clients achieve the same kind of balance, so that they are better able to make the personal transformations necessary to catapult them to new professional heights.

Taking Action

- Describe the ideal coach for your organization.
- Write down on paper your vision of your ideal coach; reflect on it and adjust it as necessary.
- Keep that ideal coach in mind as you begin to assess individual coach competencies.
- Refuse to accept anyone less than the best coach for your organization!

NOTE

1. For more information about the ICF, go to www. coachfederation.org.

APPENDIX I

Sample Coaching Participant Manual

THIS MANUAL IS PROVIDED as an example and a template that organizations can use to develop their own, to give to employees who will participate in the coaching initiative. As noted in the body of the text, each organization will have its own definition of coaching; the language provided here is intended to serve as a starting place.

NOTE

Sponsors of coaching programs should fully answer each question posed here prior to introducing the coaching initiative to those who will participate in the programs.

PREFACE

Welcome to the world of coaching! We are pleased to be working with you, and we appreciate your commitment to your professional development. Your experience working with a coach will be a unique one; the relationship you form with your coach will be one that allows you to engage in confidential and objective conversations. These conversations are focused on you and what you need to best leverage the knowledge you gain from them.

Our coaches are highly trained and skilled. In the coming weeks, you will be in contact with your coach. [Provide details about how the person being coached and his or her coach will connect. Will the coach make the initial contact, or will the person being coached do so? How will contact information be exchanged?]

You are the chief designer of your coaching experience. With that in mind, consider these benefits of working with a coach:

- To achieve clarity regarding your objectives and goals.
- To assess and improve important working relationships.
- To focus on taking effective action.
- To identify obstacles and barriers that may be holding you back.

We are deeply committed to making your coaching experience fulfilling and beneficial to you and your organization. We look forward to getting your feedback once you have completed your coaching program.

Sincerely,
Your Coaching Services Group

Contact Information

If you are participating in an organizational coaching initiative, please fill in the information below so you have all of the information handy if you have questions about the program.

CORPORATE SPONSOR

Name _____

Telephone _____

Email _____

Name _____

Telephone _____

Email _____

FREQUENTLY ASKED QUESTIONS

Coaching is not a spectator sport. A productive coaching relationship begins with two people with fires in their bellies: one who wants desperately to move forward and another who yearns to help that person make the journey.

—James Belasco, Coaching for Leadership

WHAT IS COACHING?

Coaching is a deliberate process that uses focused conversations to create an environment for individual growth, purposeful action, and sustained improvement. Coaching is a one-on-one process based on a relationship between an individual and a coach, who formulate specific objectives and goals that are focused on developing potential, improving professional relationships, and enhancing performance. Coaching uses a formalized yet personalized approach that integrates proven techniques for change with behavioral knowledge and practical experience. Coaching breaks down barriers to help achieve greater levels of accomplishment. It is a process of self-leadership that enables people to gain clarity about who they are, what they are doing, and why they are doing it.

The one-on-one coaching relationship is used in conjunction with Web-enabled technology to:

- Unlock an individual's potential and maximize his or her performance.
- Challenge and aid individuals in taking effective action.
- Lead individuals to an understanding of the essence of themselves (their character) to achieve personal and professional satisfaction.

WHAT IS A COACH?

A coach is a success broker and partner—a dedicated professional who specializes in developing and helping others excel. A coach is part mentor, advisor, sounding board, and devil's advocate. A coach creates a safe environment in which both parties can share insights and information, untangle the causes of limitations (sometimes self-imposed), and identify effective methods to practice new approaches. As an unbiased third party, a coach uses a variety of methods to help clients attain greater clarity; learn new, or upgrade existing, skill sets; and achieve greater job satisfaction and an improved quality of life.

Personal versus Professional Coaches

- Personal coaches have as their goal the personal achievement and success of the client.
- Professional coaches have as their goal the professional achievement and success of the client, whether it is an individual or an organization. Professional coaches may also be called organizational coaches and executive coaches.

WHAT DOES A COACH DO?

Coaches:

- Create a safe environment in which a person being coached can see his- or herself more clearly. Coaches listen, ask focused questions, reflect back, challenge, and acknowledge the client.
- Assist the person being coached in understanding how to grow and thrive, by championing, advocating, and standing for that person's best self.
- Guide the person being coached in setting an agenda so that he or she can grow naturally and comfortably.
- Encourage intentional thought, action, and behavior changes when the person being coached is reluctant to do so.
- Inject enough dynamic tension into the coaching process to compel the person being coached to take action and effect positive change.

Coaches also:

- Identify gaps between where the person being coached is and where that person needs or wants to be.
- Help the person being coached develop a strong personal action plan to close those gaps and hold the individual rigorously accountable to that plan.
- Understand and anticipate obstacles that will slow the progress of the person being coached (including personal limitations) and strategize with the person to overcome them.
- Institute the structure necessary to ensure a sustained commitment for both parties.
- Maintain the client's focus and vision, to help him or her remember has been defined as most important.

WHAT DOES A COACH NOT DO?

Coaches do not:

- *Consult*: A consultant is a person with specific expertise hired to share that expertise with individuals or organizations.

Coaching, in contrast, is focused on drawing the expertise and answers from the client.

- *Counsel*: Coaching effects achievement; counseling effects healing. Coaching effects action; counseling effects understanding. Coaching promotes creativity; counseling seeks to resolve. Coaching is about the future; counseling is about the past and how it impacts the present.

HOW DOES COACHING WORK?

Coaching comprises a series of interactive conversations, generally scheduled on a regular or periodic basis. The conversations take place either in a confidential face-to-face meeting or via telephone.

You and your coach should discuss how to make between-session contact—whether to use voice mail or email or to schedule brief check-in appointments.

WHAT IF I HAVE TO MISS AN APPOINTMENT?

It is common for a professional service provider to require a 24-hour notice for rescheduling an appointment; we request the same courtesy.

IS COACHING CONFIDENTIAL?

Yes. Our trained and experienced coaches understand the need for complete confidentiality. They are bound by ethics agreements, which include strict confidentiality, and are dedicated to your advancement, achievement, and success. They understand the importance of trust in the coaching relationship.

IS THERE ANYTHING I CAN'T DISCUSS WITH MY COACH?

You can talk with your coach about anything that is affecting you, and confidentiality will be maintained unless it violates company policy. Company policy usually requires reporting the following: harassment, discrimination, and illegal activity. If you share any of these issues, your coach is required to report the information, and your human resources representative will be contacted as well.

WHAT IF I DON'T LIKE MY COACH?

Coaches know that not every client and coach are a good fit. If either you or your coach feels that you are mismatched, bring it up and talk about it. If a change is needed, you'll be connected with a different coach for the remaining sessions. If necessary, you may want to talk with your corporate sponsor about this.

DOES MY COACH REPLACE MY MANAGER?

No. Your manager is still your manager and plays a vital role in your professional development. During your coaching relationship, your coach may suggest that you schedule time with your manager to discuss situations or issues as they arise, for your benefit. Your coach will not discuss anything with your manager unless it is mutually agreed upon by you and your coach; nor will there be any contact between your coach and your manager about the nature of your coaching relationship unless you initiate it.

HOW CAN I GET THE MOST OUT OF COACHING?

First and foremost, keep your appointments, and protect your coaching time from intrusions. It is your responsibility to call your coach at the scheduled time. Other suggestions include:

- Ask questions. Share your doubts, concerns, and impressions with your coach.
- Remember that you are the client. Ask for what you want. Tell your coach how he or she can best serve you. If your

coach isn't asking enough questions, is talking too much or too fast, or is doing something that annoys you, tell him or her immediately! Think of the coaching relationship as an alliance, whose sole purpose is to serve you.

- Be willing to stretch your thinking and attitudes during your coaching sessions. Remember, this is a safe place to process the experience and learn from it.
- Be willing to share your coaching experience with colleagues, and be willing to listen to theirs!

Additional Questions to Consider

- What's in it for me?
- What's in it for my organization?
- If I want to learn more about coaching, where can I go?
- How much time will it take (weekly and by contract)?

APPENDIX II

Sample Coaching Impact Report

[Client Company]

Impact Evaluation of the
[Coaching Company]
Coaching Intervention

Executive Summary Report

[Date]

Study Designed and Completed by:
[Research Company Name]

INTRODUCTION

[Client] Company engaged the [Coaching] Company to provide a series of coaching sessions for 67 of its staff members. The participants in the coaching process included all managers, from the executive level to district sales managers. This intervention began early in [date] and concluded for most participants in [date]. It was the express intention of the coaching intervention to deliver results against key business goals. The purpose of this impact evaluation was to determine whether those results were produced, why and by whom, and, if not, why not. The report captures these data.

BACKGROUND AND METHODOLOGY

The investigators used a "success case" methodology, which is described in detail in the full report.

Key Findings

1. **The coaching intervention has produced significant business and economic impact.**

   Overall, the investigators are confident that Client Company has achieved total impact in the millions. The immediate return on investment will be in the 10 to 1 range. The long-term return will be even higher.

   Specifically, the investigators found abundant evidence that this intervention contributed directly to specific KRAs:

   - *Top-performing staff have been retained.* Retaining a top-performing account executive and a district manager saved the company in excess of $100,000 and kept current revenues and customer satisfaction at very high levels.
   - *A positive work environment has been created.* Managers working more effectively with their reports have helped them focus on strategic account development, thus increasing sales results in excess of $250,000.

- *Revenue increased with the improved productivity of formerly average ACE performers.** The company earned in excess of $75,000.
- *There was reduced erosion in customer base, revenues, and customer satisfaction.* This was effected because territories could be staffed more quickly when vacancies occurred, thus saving the company in excess of $100,000.

The investigators are confident that Client Company has achieved, at a very conservative level, a 10-to-1 return on investment. Simply by adding the four impact profiles presented in this report, a 10-to-1 return rate is achieved. Note that five additional impact stories are not included in this report but had similar economic impact; and 32 high-impact participants not interviewed would also push this return rate substantially higher.

2. **Sponsorship of this initiative at the executive level of leadership in the organization made the business impact more likely.**

   Prior to the start of and during the coaching initiative, there was excellent sponsorship and communication about the importance of coaching for the individuals and the organization.

3. **The timing of this intervention contributed to the high level of business impact.**

   The coaching intervention, undertaken during a time of changing organizational structure, reporting relationships, and sales process, increased the business impact.

---

*A revenue increase may seem to be an inaccurate conclusion here given Client Company's year-to-date revenue levels. In fact, however, this conclusion is not about Client Company revenues but about the way in which the coaching intervention helped managers work more effectively with targeted individuals to improve their productivity. The more accurate question would be: "How much further below plan might Client Company have been had the coaching initiative not been in place?"

4. **Participant openness to the coaching process made a decided difference in the personal and business impact that was achieved.**

   Those who reported the highest levels of personal and business impact were excited by the coaching opportunity being provided by their company.

5. **Significant business and personal alignment between individuals and within teams occurred as a result of the coaching intervention.**

   Individuals being coached became more aware of how actions connected with their key responsibility areas were linked to organizational success.

6. **This intervention demonstrated how people and performance can be positively changed using a process, rather than an event.**

   The coaching process allowed participants to work on new behaviors over time, creating shifts that otherwise might not have occurred in a two-day classroom event. Participants were also able to integrate lessons learned in coaching into their jobs.

7. **A neutral, third-party coach proved valuable at several levels.**

   Participants in this intervention described how they talked with their coaches about issues they had difficulty raising with their managers/reports. This process served to bring managers and reports together, helped them align on key business goals, and brought about more effective working relationships.

8. **The intervention will have long-lasting impact on Client Company's people and business.**

   Fully 92 percent of all survey respondents indicated that they learned coaching techniques they are using now with their direct reports.

9. **There was confusion on the part of participants as to whether they were working with a coach or a consultant.**

At the beginning of the process, many participants wanted the coach to tell them what to do in response to a need they had.

10. **The process did not have a clear exit strategy.**

Many participants were uncertain about the next steps, if any, that followed their 10 coaching sessions.

RECOMMENDATIONS

The following are recommended actions the Client Company can take to extend and enhance the business impact of future coaching interventions.

1. **Allow for flexible scheduling of the coaching sessions.**

A significant number of participants found that weekly coaching sessions made the process seem rushed, as opposed to driven by need or circumstance. All agreed that the first two to four sessions should be scheduled closer together to help build a foundation for the process and the coaching relationship. They also suggested that succeeding sessions be scheduled by mutual agreement between coach and participant.

2. **Ensure that participants' managers fully support the coaching process.**

Interview data suggest that manager involvement with participants during and after the coaching sessions was relatively low. With greater manager engagement, the level of business impact would have been higher. This applies to any human performance improvement initiative that Client Company implements.

3. **Communicate clearly what participants should expect from the process.**

   Both Client Company and the Coaching Company share the responsibility for communicating with participants how the process works, who does what, and what they can expect as outcomes. In this case, it took many participants two or more sessions to figure out that coaching was not consulting or counseling.

4. **Provide participants with a clear exit strategy for the process.**

   A process with no clear exit strategy precludes closure. Participants were left wondering, "What happens next?" Client Company and Coaching Company should discuss ideas for closure, which could include anything from a celebration of achievements to additional coaching sessions.

Bibliography

BOOKS

Bacon, Terry, and Karen Spear. *Adaptive Coaching.* Palo Alto, CA: Davies Black Publishing, 2003.

Berman-Fortgang, Laura. *Now What: 90 Days to a New Life Direction.* New York: Penguin Group, 2004.

Blanchard, Kenneth, Thad Lacinak, Chuck Thompkins, and Jim Ballard. *Whale Done: The Power of Positive Relationships.* New York: The Free Press, 2002.

Blanchard, Scott, and Madeleine Homan. *Leverage Your Best, Ditch the Rest.* New York: HarperCollins, 2004.

Brinkerhoff, Robert O. *The Success Case Method: Find Out Quickly What's Working and What's Not.* San Francisco: Berrett-Koehler, 2003.

Buckingham, Marcus. *The One Thing You Need to Know about Great Managing, Great Leadership, and Sustained Individual Success.* New York: Free Press, 2005.

Coach U. *Coach U's Essential Coaching Tools.* Hoboken, NJ: John Wiley & Sons, Inc., 2005.

Collins, Jim. *Good to Great: Why Some Companies Make the Leap . . . and Others Don't.* New York: HarperCollins, 2001.

Crane, Thomas. *The Heart of Coaching.* San Diego, CA: FTY Press, 1998.

Fairley, Stephen G., and Chris E. Stout. *Getting Started in Personal and Executive Coaching: How to Create a Thriving Coaching Practice.* Hoboken, NJ: John Wiley & Sons, Inc., 2004.

Gallwey, W. Timothy. *The Inner Game of Tennis.* New York: Random House, 1974.

Hargrove, Robert. *Masterful Coaching.* San Francisco: Jossey-Bass Pfeiffer, 2003.

Kinlaw, Dennis. *Coaching for Commitment.* San Francisco: Jossey-Bass Pfeiffer, 1999.

Lencioni, Patrick. *The Five Dysfunctions of a Team*. San Francisco: Jossey-Bass Pfeiffer, 2002.

O'Neill, Mary Beth. *Executive Coaching with Backbone and Heart: A Systems Approach to Engaging Leaders with Their Challenges*. San Francisco: Jossey-Bass Pfeiffer, 2000.

Scott, Susan. *Achieving Success at Work & in Life, One Conversation at a Time*. New York: Penguin USA, 2002.

Seashore, Charles N., Edith Whitfield Seashore, and Gerald M. Weinberg. *What Did You Say? The Art of Giving and Receiving Feedback*. Columbia, MD: Bingham House Books, 1997.

Switzler, Al, Joseph Grenny, and Ron McMillan. *Crucial Conversations: Tools for Talking When Stakes Are High*. New York: McGraw-Hill, 2002.

Whitmore, John. *Coaching for Performance*. London: Nicholas Brealey Publishing Limited, 1992.

Zigarmi, Drea, Ken Blanchard, and Patricia Zigarmi. *Leadership and the One-Minute Manager*. New York: HarperCollins, 1985.

ARTICLES

Business Wire Editors/Technology Writers. "Executive Coaching Yields Return on Investment of Almost Six Times Its Cost, Says Study." *Business Wire* (January 4, 2001); www.findarticles.com/p/articles/mi_m0EIN/is_2001_Jan_4/ai_68725844.

Grant, Anthony. "Keynote Presentation, International Coach Federation Conference Symposium on Research and Coaching." Denver, CO, November 2003.

McGovern, Joy, et al. "Maximizing the Impact of Executive Coaching: Behavioral Change, Organizational Outcomes and Return on Investment." *The Manchester Review*, Vol. 6, 2001: 1–9.

Michelman, Paul. "Do You Need an Executive Coach?" *Harvard Management Update*, 2004: 3–4.

Rackham, Neil. "Measuring the Impact of Sales Training," *American Society for Training and Development*, Vol. 2, 1997: 89–101.

Ram, Charan, and Geoffrey Colvin. "Why CEOs Fail," *Fortune* (June 21, 1999): 78.

Sandstrom, Jeannine, Linda Miller, and Bob Johnson. "Coaching Dialogue: A View inside Coaching Organizations." *The International Journal of Coaching in Organizations*, 2005: 25–35.

Von Hoffman, Constantine. "Coaching: The Ten Killer Myths." *Harvard Management Update*, 1999: 3–4.

Index

21047261R00145

Made in the USA
San Bernardino, CA
04 May 2015